MW01194918

BEYOND THE
WORK PRODUCT

BEYOND THE WORK PRODUCT

A Guide to Relationship-Driven Transactional Lawyering

RACHEL LANDY

AMERICAN**BAR**ASSOCIATION

Solo, Small Firm and
General Practice Division

Cover design by Amanda Fry/ABA Publishing.

The materials contained herein represent the opinions of the authors and/or the editors, and should not be construed to be the views or opinions of the law firms or companies with whom such persons are in partnership with, associated with, or employed by, nor of the American Bar Association or the Solo, Small Firm and General Practice Division, unless adopted pursuant to the bylaws of the Association.

Nothing contained in this book is to be considered as the rendering of legal advice for specific cases, and readers are responsible for obtaining such advice from their own legal counsel. This book is intended for educational and informational purposes only.

© 2021 American Bar Association. All rights reserved.

No part of this publication may be reproduced, stored in a retrieval system, or transmitted in any form or by any means, electronic, mechanical, photocopying, recording, or otherwise, without the prior written permission of the publisher. For permission contact the ABA Copyrights & Contracts Department, copyright@ americanbar.org, or complete the online form at http://www.americanbar.org /utility/reprint.html.

Printed in the United States of America.

25 24 23 22   5 4 3

Library of Congress Cataloging-in-Publication Data

Names: Landy, Rachel E., author.
Title: Beyond the work product: a guide to relationship-driven transactional lawyering/Rachel E. Landy.
Description: Chicago, Illinois: American Bar Association, [2021] |
  Includes index. | Summary: "This book is designed to prepare business attorneys (and particularly, law students and new attorneys) for a successful law practice by providing a framework for effective and efficient lawyering, with an emphasis on building relationships and trust with clients so that, in spite of cheaper alternatives, they will keep coming back for more"–Provided by publisher.
Identifiers: LCCN 2020046441 (print) | LCCN 2020046442 (ebook) |
  ISBN 9781641058407 (board) | ISBN 9781641058414 (ebook)
Subjects: LCSH: Attorney and client–United States. | Lawyers–United States. |
  Business enterprises–Law and legislation–United States.
Classification: LCC KF311.L36 2021 (print) | LCC KF311 (ebook) |
  DDC 340.023/73–dc23
LC record available at https://lccn.loc.gov/2020046441
LC ebook record available at https://lccn.loc.gov/2020046442

Discounts are available for books ordered in bulk. Special consideration is given to state bars, CLE programs, and other bar-related organizations. Inquire at Book Publishing, ABA Publishing, American Bar Association, 321 N. Clark Street, Chicago, Illinois 60654-7598.

www.shopABA.org

Contents

Introduction

Welcome to *Beyond the Work Product.* If you are reading this, then you are either preparing for or have begun a career as an attorney, which is no small feat, particularly when the legal industry is undergoing a lot of change. Hourly billing rates continue to increase, while clients seek to pay less, or not "by the hour" at all. At the same time, technology innovators have pegged law services as a target for automation, potentially undermining the value of a legal education and career. Faced with the possibility of having your chosen profession relegated to artificial intelligence, it is easy to get discouraged. But don't be. There is still immeasurable value in legal training. This book will help you approach your work in a relationship-minded way, allowing you to sustain a practice despite these increasing obstacles.

This book is designed to prepare business attorneys (and particularly law students and new attorneys)[1] for a successful law practice by providing a framework for effective and efficient lawyering, with an emphasis on building relationships and trust with clients so that, in spite of cheaper alternatives, they will keep coming back for more. Think of this as a "process-focused" instead of "outcome-focused" approach, with more consideration placed on each step of the lawyering process, not simply delivering the best work product possible. Whether you are

---

[1] As described later in this introduction, this book is geared toward business lawyers but can be useful for litigators as well.

at a big firm, a small firm, or a solo practice,[2] seeing lawyering as a relationship-driven job will help you to build a sustainable practice and, I'm optimistic to say, enjoy the work a bit more.

Too often, "business development" is separated from actual law practice. "Business development" focuses on networking events and expensive meals to land new clients, which are kept wholly distinct from delivering client service. Once a client has signed onto an engagement letter with the firm, they are often passed on to associates to do the actual legwork on their projects. These two work streams need not—and should not—be so detached from each other. Attorneys should always be thinking of how to develop more business from the clients they have already landed, and every project with every client provides that opportunity. If that opportunity is squandered, however, then the client will go to another firm or try out new legal technology. The framework provided in this book seeks to merge the two functions—practice and business development—so that lawyering builds the relationships needed to further develop the business.

Focusing on relationship building is fundamental to sustaining a practice because in the face of less expensive, and more automated, solutions, clients will become increasingly sensitive to costs and look for client service that does not break the bank. A successful lawyer provides that service in a cost-conscious manner, while engendering trust, fostering institutional knowledge, and managing the emotional toll that comes with negotiating difficult deals. These attributes define the human aspects of advocacy and cannot be software-engineered away. Good work product should be an end result of a thoughtful, collaborative approach to drafting, but not the only result.

Getting Comfortable Talking—and Thinking—about Costs

We're only two pages into the book and I have already mentioned costs, fees, and bills several times. If you are just starting out in your career, then you might be a bit uncomfortable. You might be thinking "my ethics teacher talked about 'zealous representation' and 'competence'

---

[2] Much of this book includes how to manage dynamics with colleagues and other lawyers within a firm. If you are a solo practitioner, those provisions may not be directly applicable to you, but the same principles apply to any lawyer you might collaborate with and hopefully provide helpful insight on how to approach professional relationships generally.

as the primary ethical duties of a lawyer and did not say anything about what a client can and cannot afford." It is true that your ethical duties are paramount to lawyering. However, maximizing revenues and minimizing expenses are also imperative to your client's ability to build a business—and *you are an expense.* That inherent tension in the job—how to provide the best legal services possible in the least amount of time (i.e., the most cost-effective way)—can be difficult to reconcile, and how to handle that tension is seldom taught in law school. Yet, one of the most difficult conversations that lawyers in private practice (whether a solo practitioner or senior associate at the largest law firm) have with clients is about their bill. Many lawyers are more comfortable telling a client that they are taking an unreasonable position in a negotiation they cannot win with a counterparty than having a direct discussion about how much a project will cost. In the midst of trying to provide legal advice and good client service, the bill is an unwanted reminder that the attorney-client relationship is also a business relationship.

As such, every conversation with a client about the bill has the possibility of introducing friction into the relationship. While a partner is typically on the front lines for those exchanges, the existence and outcome of those billing discussions will certainly trickle down to all team members, and if you are the lawyer who is "billing too much," it will affect your marketability within the firm and to clients. Moreover, good junior lawyers become good midlevel attorneys, who may become good senior associates, and thus end up taking and managing those calls themselves. For this reason, I stress continually throughout this book that all private practice attorneys should strive to provide effective *and* efficient[3] legal advice. Be vigilant in setting a client's expectations about costs, but also aim to provide every client with significantly more value from a transaction (which includes the counsel and advice that you provide, as well as the deliverable) than they are being asked to pay.

Of course, being conscious about the bill does not equate to providing sloppy work product or half-baked legal advice. Rather, it means exercising good judgment to know when enough is enough for a particular project. I refer to this skill—the ability to put the right amount of effort into a project, given the client's business and sophistication and the nature of the project—as "calibration." This book provides numerous different ways to help you calibrate for your projects, but the first step is to understand that perfect work product does not always equate

---

[3] As further set out in Chapter 2, "efficient" is lawyer-speak for "less expensive."

to a happy client, particularly if perfect work costs several thousand dollars when "good enough" would have been half that. Many junior lawyers who are trained to focus solely on producing perfect work product, regardless of the time or expense it takes, often struggle in this area. As good as their work product is, those associates also generate the most client complaints: "Why did so and so spend eighteen hours on a three-page agreement?" "Why did this form nondisclosure agreement cost $6,000?" The associates who can calibrate well are the ones that clients want to continue working with (and complain less about). A pleased client with the properly calibrated (albeit not necessarily perfect, but good enough) work product makes for better business than the perfect work product delivered to a client bruised by an overlawyered process. Calibration can set you up for a long-lasting career: clients and colleagues will want to work with you because your work style is unlikely to introduce additional business friction into client relationships.

A Book about Relationships

I remember the first time that a client referred to me in an email as simply "legal": "Our legal is copied." I felt dehumanized. I was just a job function that was tied to a line item on the client's budget. I had no name. I could be swapped out for any other attorney. At that point, I decided that in order for me to enjoy my job—the long hours, late-night phone calls, urgent demands, and adversarial conversations—I needed to find a way to be more than just "legal" to my clients. I wanted my clients to see *me* (and not just any lawyer) as part of their team, as a trusted advisor who was invested in their long-term success. So, I set out to ensure that each drafting project I undertook for a client was also an investment in our relationship. I refused to be relegated to a cost center. This book reflects how I refined that skill (vis-à-vis both clients and colleagues) over my several years in law practice.

This book is written as a step-by-step guide for lawyers to approach drafting assignments in a manner that builds these relationships, delivers effective and efficient work product, and creates a feedback loop of institutional knowledge and trust that cannot be automated or commoditized. I was a technology transactions lawyer (and not a litigator), and this book is geared toward business lawyers—that is, those working on transactional projects (be it as a corporate, real estate, tax, employment, or commercial attorney). Litigators may find value in this book, however, by gaining an understanding of how a contractual relationship comes together before it falls apart and lands on their desks. Moreover, for litigators who draft settlement agreements, the principles set forth in Chapters 3 (relating to ethical obligations), 5, and 6 (relating to drafting techniques) are equally applicable.[4]

To illuminate the concepts described, I primarily use emerging companies ("start-ups") as examples, rather than large public corporations. I do this for a few reasons:

1. Clients with limited legal budgets, like start-ups, are the most likely to dump traditional bill-by-the-hour private practice representation for cheaper, technology-driven alternatives.

2. Start-up communities (particularly in the technology sector) continue to grow all over the country. Industries that were once exclusive to Silicon Valley now have hubs in New York, Austin, Miami, San Diego, Los Angeles, Denver, and more.

3. Working with smaller companies provides the most opportunity to show how value can be added by a good outside counsel. Small companies are more likely to lean heavily on their outside lawyers for input on both business and legal issues. This provides great opportunities for lawyers to partner with their clients on big-picture issues and long-term thinking.

4. Lawyers who are not practicing at traditionally "big" firms are likely to have smaller companies for clients.

Before we dive in, I want to quickly sketch out what this book is not:

1. *The nuts and bolts of "how to draft a contract."* Provided in Chapter 2 is a baseline overview of the main components of a contract, which every lawyer should understand in order to have a productive conversation with a client or colleague about a drafting project, and to effectively represent a client. For detailed guidance on how every provision of a contract can and/or should be drafted, I recommend Tina Stark's books (specifically, "*Negotiating and Drafting Contract Boilerplate* and *Drafting Contracts: How and Why Lawyers Do What They Do*). If you are still a student, seek out a "contract drafting" skills-based course if your law school offers one.

2. *A negotiation guide.* In Chapter 8, guidelines are set forth for how to approach negotiations to effectively and efficiently represent your client, but specific advocacy techniques to use when negotiating against an adverse party are not covered. I recommend participating in negotiation clinics (many law firms and law schools have them) and reading *Getting to Yes* by Roger Fisher and William Ury.

---

[4] However, be mindful of the fundamental differences between business contracts and settlement contracts. Notably, settlement contracts memorialize the end of a relationship, while business contracts are just the beginning.

Throughout this book, we work with a fictional client, Fitness Feet, whom you will meet in the next chapter. Subsequent chapters review the basic components of a contract, the steps you should take when you first receive an assignment, and the drafting and negotiation processes, with each point highlighted by real-world examples and exercises for you to test out the proposed strategy.

I'll let you in on a little secret: the best part of being a transactional lawyer is not the money or the occasional intellectual exercise. It is building connections, getting to know your clients, and being part of a problem-solving team. When you start seeing your work as an opportunity to bond with people in that capacity, instead of as a robotic contract-drafting function, you might even start to have fun. So, with all of that in mind, let's begin!

Chapter 1

Our Client: Fitness Feet

You are sitting in your office at the beginning of your second week at your first job out of law school, at a very prestigious firm, Landy Law LLP. You are fortunate to have landed a gig at a firm that represents venture-backed technology companies, which, given your pre–law school career as a software engineer, fits neatly with your background and is exactly what you wanted to specialize in when you started law school. You finished orientation, learned the ins and outs of time entry (and how to keep track of your time), fumbled around enough with the contract management system to get a general sense of how it works, and took your assistant out for coffee (a mid-level associate warned you not to overlook the importance of building that key relationship). After three long years of law school, you are excited to be a "real lawyer." A senior associate who recently lateraled from another firm, Ashley Associate, gently taps on your door to get your attention before walking in.

"Hey there. Welcome to the firm. Got time to help with a new client?"

"Of course! What can I do?" you eagerly reply.

"Okay, great. We have a client, Fitness Feet, which makes a wearable fitness tracker that measures your heart rate and other fitness stuff by taking readings from the ankle. Supposedly there is some science that makes that work. They're going to be doing some commercial deals and hopefully a financing, and I could use some help getting the agreements off the ground. The first one we need is a super short partnership agreement between them and a gym that is going to give away some gift cards for Fitness Feet's ankle trackers to its members in exchange for the gym featuring the trackers in email marketing and social media. They're excited about this and will probably want to get the deal done ASAP. I think the gym is called Easy Exercise, but you should confirm with the client. There's also a manufacturing agreement in the pipeline that we'll start another work stream for. I'll introduce you to our point person, Casey, who runs most of the business deals. Casey is not a lawyer, so don't be afraid to do a bit of hand-holding. Make sure I'm in the loop and copied on the emails. They can be a bit demanding, but if you keep them updated on timelines and don't leave them hanging, they won't get upset. Oh, and since they're venture-backed and looking to do another round soon, they're pretty mindful about their legal budget so don't go crazy billing on this. Feel free to come to me with any questions. Need anything else to get started?"

Our Framework

Throughout this book, we are going to be working with Fitness Feet on the deals that Ashley mentioned (and others). I developed Fitness Feet based on the hundreds of emerging company clients I worked with over several years in practice. As such, the dialogues with Casey from Fitness Feet you see throughout the chapters reflect the kinds of conversations I had with similar companies and are indicative of the types of communications you should get used to having with clients.

Like many start-up clients, Fitness Feet does not have an in-house legal team. So, you will be working directly with the businessperson, Casey. Early stage companies, which are the most likely to be sensitive to legal fees, often do not have in-house counsel. Even the clients who do have in-house legal teams may need for you to talk directly to their business team if they are handing off a deal to you. Therefore, getting used to working with nonlawyers is a significant part of building a practice. Working with nonlawyers and other business folks can work to your benefit if you invest in building a relationship and partnering with the client rather than treating them like a revenue center: they will treat you less like an expense. On the other hand, if you do not use your projects and interactions to demonstrate a commitment to a long-lasting relationship and the development of institutional knowledge and instead act as a mere scrivener, then you will be first on the list of budget items to cut.

Each chapter includes exercises so that you can take a stab at tackling the issue at hand using the guidelines provided. Except where noted, sample responses to the exercises are provided at the end of each chapter. Also included are drafts of language for emails and suggestions that I recommend considering as you begin to build your practice.

Examples of emails or contract language are set off with arrows and italics. You will also notice there are certain key phrases I use over and over again. Following is a quick key to what those terms mean:

1. *Calibrate:* Calibrating, as you have already learned, means exercising good judgment to know when enough is enough for a particular project, given the client's business and sophistication and the nature of the project. It is the ability to recognize that the practice of law is not "one size fits all."

2. *Efficiency:* When I speak about being efficient in working on a project, I mean that you are finding ways to spend less time to get to a good result. Less time means less money for the client, so when talking to a client, "efficient" is really just a euphemism for "less expensive."

3. *Future headache:* A "future headache" is a foreseeable issue that will arise unless you put in the right amount of effort now to avoid it. Future headaches come in a variety of flavors and can arise from how you, as a lawyer, manage your own workload, as well as how you advise your client on their decision-making. "Avoid future headaches" is a helpful mantra to repeat to yourself over and over again. Write it on a Post-it note and stick it on your computer monitor. Set an alarm on your phone for every Monday morning to remind you of this important mindset. Your ability to avoid future headaches will be instrumental to your success and enable you to work more efficiently.

4. *Negotiation capital:* Negotiation capital translates to how much juice you have to leverage in a negotiation. Think of this capital as funds in a bank account that are withdrawn as they are spent (but can also be earned back).

Last, here is a quick note on pronouns. I use the term "client" to refer to both the company (i.e., Fitness Feet) and the client's representative that you work with (i.e., Casey). "They," as used throughout the book, refers to either.

This book is meant to be friendly and interactive, so please take a pen or a highlighter (whether digital or real) to the pages as you see appropriate and have fun.

Chapter 2

Understanding How a Contract Fits Together

A lbert Einstein reportedly said, "If you can't explain it simply, you don't understand it well enough." It is for that reason that we are starting our journey with a bit of academia. It is extremely difficult for anyone to teach that which they do not themselves fully comprehend— and in a world being reshaped by technology and automation, what stands out to clients (and keeps clients coming back) is when you take the time to explain key legal concepts in a nonlawyer, plain English manner, and ensure they understand. A recurring theme of this book is that taking the time to educate your clients demonstrates to them that you are invested in their long-term success and vision, and willing to partner with them to achieve their goals. It shows that you are more than just a scribe.

In order to articulate to clients the implications of agreeing to the different terms of a contract, a lawyer must first have a fundamental comprehension of how an agreement fits together. Then, that lawyer can turn around and translate the applicable legal and contractual concepts in accessible, business-friendly language.

This is where the rubber meets the road in law practice. Understanding the various components of an agreement is fundamental to being able to advise a client and draft a good contract. Yet, law school classes tend to glaze over (at best) how doctrinal concepts show up in practice. The first time a partner asked me "what the consideration was" in a deal

I was working on, my head nearly exploded. I truly did not think I would ever hear that term in "real life," but I did—many times over. In fact, I explained "consideration" and why it is important to get it right to dozens of clients and had many conversations with colleagues about whether a proposed exchange met the prevailing "peppercorn"[1] legal standard.

Don't get me wrong—learning doctrine and how to read case law is valuable. But in many cases, the most transferrable skill from lecture courses is not what the specific law is, but how to think about law, generally. Issue-spotting is an absolutely necessary skill for any lawyer. However, no matter how well a lawyer learns to issue-spot, the full value of law school will not be realized unless that lawyer can also translate basic legal concepts into language their clients will understand and appreciate. This chapter aims to help you develop that skill as it pertains to business contracts by reviewing the basic components of an agreement and focusing on why those components matter to both the drafter (you) and clients. As we undertake this exercise, we begin to build on our Fitness Feet example, as well as look at some hypotheticals from other contexts.

Contract provisions can be loosely divided into three large buckets: (1) performance covenants, (2) risk-shifting provisions, and (3) what I refer to as the "rules of the road." A good business lawyer must know how these different parts of a contract function and work together in order to effectively and efficiently draft, advocate, and negotiate. As noted earlier, this knowledge includes the ability to skillfully translate each legal concept into "plain English" for clients and help those clients understand the promises they are making (and their implications). Lawyers should assume that their clients are not trained in reading contractual language (even when not written in formal "legalese") or understanding how legal terms will impact business operations. This is true even if the client is a lawyer. As outside counsel, you are being hired to facilitate their understanding and translate their business deal into appropriate contract language. In-house lawyers often have very full plates and off-load things to outside counsel because they do not have the time to focus on a particular deal.

Perfecting the ability to articulate legal concepts in digestible language is critical to building the trust that characterizes, and is fundamental to, any long-standing attorney-client relationship. Being able to foster your clients' deeper understanding of their business deals is a value-add that cannot be replicated by technology (or less informed lawyers).

I review each bucket of contract provisions in the sections that follow, including best practices for drafting, and use several exercises and

---

[1] Whitney v. Stearns, 16 Me. 394, 397 (1839).

examples to illustrate the different points. My goal is for you to understand why each concept matters and be able to articulate that information to your clients.

Covenants of Performance

In General

Covenants are, generally speaking, what each party promises to do under the contract.[2] Some covenants are fundamental to the business relationship: the parties have come together because each wants the other to do *something*: pay money, perform at an event, provide services, grant equity, deliver content or work product, maintain the confidentiality of certain materials, approve or reject uses of a logo, manufacture a product, supply a component part, grant a license, and so on. Other covenants are used to further operationalize and tease out the details of performance for each party.

Consideration

One meaningful example of a covenant required in every contract is the promise to exchange consideration, or something of value. Consideration, as you may recall from your contracts course, is required to have an enforceable contract,[3] and while it need not be much, it must be *something* (i.e., at least a peppercorn).[4] How the parties agree to exchange consideration is usually through a pair of covenants—an obligation on the part of each party to provide something.

When drafting these covenants, the word "consideration" does not need to be used unless it will not be obvious to a reader what exactly constitutes the consideration. Take Fitness Feet, for example. As Ashley alerted us, there is a manufacturing agreement in the pipeline for the client. Assume Fitness Feet is paying that manufacturer, Sporty Supply, $10 per fitness tracker, and Sporty Supply is manufacturing and delivering the trackers to Fitness Feet. In that case, the reader will understand right away what each party is contributing as consideration: $10 per tracker in Fitness Feet's case, and the manufactured trackers in Sporty Supply's case.

If the consideration is not easily discernible, however, then it can be helpful to "recite" (i.e., specify) the consideration for the sake of your

---

[2] 8 JOSEPH M. PERILLO ET AL., CORBIN ON CONTRACTS § 30.12 (rev. ed. 2009); COMMERCIAL CONTRACTS: STRATEGIES FOR NEGOTIATING AND DRAFTING, § 2.03[F] (Vladimir R. Rossman & Morton Moskin eds., 2009).

[3] Restatement (Second) of Contracts § 1 (AM. LAW INST.) (1981).

[4] Whitney, 16 M. at 6.

reader and any court required to interpret the contract. Consider Fitness Feet's other deal, with Easy Exercise: Easy Exercise will give out fifty gift cards for Fitness Feet's trackers to its members in exchange for Easy Exercise providing Fitness Feet with some promotional support on social media and in email marketing. You might say, "As consideration for the publicity and promotional opportunities that Easy Exercise provides to Fitness Feet under this Agreement, Fitness Feet will give to Easy Exercise fifty gift cards (each worth the retail value of a single fitness tracker) to distribute to Easy Exercise members." By making clear the consideration is the exchange of the gift cards (from Fitness Feet) and publicity (from Easy Exercise), if the contract is ever challenged in a court as unenforceable for lack of consideration, the nonchallenging party can point convincingly to this sentence as evidence of an intentional exchange of consideration.

The parties' promises to exchange the applicable consideration are important covenants. Yet, clients will occasionally come to you with a "deal" that has no apparent consideration. If you are concerned that your client has brought to you one of those arrangements, then explain to your client that you are concerned about the lack of enforceability of the contract and brainstorm with them what sort of consideration is appropriate to include that will not blow up the deal. Typically, agreements at risk of failing for lack of consideration do not involve money changing hands, so you may need to be creative. Can one party agree to promote the other party by posting on Instagram or TikTok? Can a party provide some promotional merchandise for the other party to give away? So long as you are meeting the peppercorn standard, it is fine (and fun) to be creative when the need arises—provided that you have explained to your client why.

> **Real-World Example:** Over several years of drafting commercial contracts, my colleagues and I considered whether the following were sufficient consideration:
>
> - $1.
> - One social media post (e.g., one tweet).
> - Company "swag" (such as a beanie with the company's logo).

Identifying Covenants

In addition to the covenants relating to consideration discussed earlier, covenants include any other promises made by a party to take actions in the future under the terms of an agreement. Other than consideration, they need not be reciprocal; often, one party to an agreement has far more obligations than the other. Covenants can range from being crucial for the deal (agreeing to develop a product, for example) to being minor operational points (e.g., promising to seek approvals for use of a logo via email).

Exercise 2-1: Can You Identify the Covenants in the Following Examples?

Example A: Billy Joel ("**Performer**") will perform at Madison Square Garden on November 12, 2021, at 7:30 p.m. Madison Square Garden Productions will pay Performer $250,000 no later than three days before the performance and an additional $250,000 within three days after the performance. During the performance, Performer will perform at least four of Performer's top-ten singles (as measured by the Billboard Hot 100 charts).

Covenant 1:

_____

_____

Covenant 2:

_____

_____

Covenant 3:

_____

_____

Example B: Consultant will perform software engineering services on an internal reporting tool according to the attached Statement of Work (the "**Services**") for Fitness Feet, Inc. ("**Fitness Feet**"). Fitness Feet will pay Consultant $20 an hour for those Services, and make available senior engineering team members on a regular basis to Consultant for ongoing review and feedback.

Covenant 1:

_____

_____

Covenant 2:

_____

_____

Covenant 3:

_____

_____

Covenants may also be expressed in the negative, as promises to refrain from taking certain actions.

→ *Consultant will not incorporate any open-source software or any other software code for which the intellectual property rights are owned by a third party in its work product without Company's prior, written approval, not to be unreasonably withheld, delayed, or conditioned.*

→ *Consultant will not make any negative statements or otherwise publicly disparage Company (including on Consultant's social media feeds, whether set to "private" or not) during the term of this Agreement and for six months thereafter.*

→ *Consultant will not perform services similar to the services it is performing for Company for Company's Direct Competitors. "**Company's Direct Competitors**" means any other entity or person in the business of making, distributing, or selling products similar to Company's products, excluding any entity or person that operates a general purpose e-commerce website or department store(s) where those similar products comprise less than 50% of that website's or store(s)'s inventory.*

Exercise 2-2:

Following is an exchange between you and Fitness Feet. In the space that follows, put together a list of the covenants that will need to be reflected in the contract, based solely on the information provided. Remember that covenants can be promises both to do and not to do certain actions. Do not worry about the defined terms or the specific contract language—just get a list together of various obligations each party will undertake. Within your set of covenants, identify which relate to the exchange of consideration.

* * *

Casey sends you the following email: "Hey there, as I think Ashley mentioned to you, we have been meeting with Sporty Supply, a company that manufactures and assembles fitness gear, for the last few weeks or so about moving our manufacturing business to them. They've agreed to supply us with our standard fitness trackers for the next year at a cost of $10 per tracker. We'll issue purchase orders to Sporty every month for the trackers that we think we'll need, and then they'll send us the trackers. We'll pay on net 30 terms,[5] but they can't invoice us until we've accepted the trackers. We don't want to be on the hook to pay until after we know it's a good batch. We told them we'd send them an agreement. Can you help put together a draft?" About thirty minutes later, Casey follows up with another note: "One more thing about that Sporty agreement—we don't want them to be able to supply any of our competitors while we're under contract."

Covenant 1:

_____

_____

Covenant 2:

_____

_____

Covenant 3:

_____

_____

Covenant 4:

_____

_____

Covenant 5:

_____

_____

Covenant 6:

_____

_____

---

[5] "Net 30" (or 60, 90, etc.) is common shorthand that means a company will pay within thirty days of the date of the invoice.

Drafting Covenants

Covenants are, by definition, obligations to be performed *in the future*, whether right after the agreement is signed or weeks or months down the line (with one notable exception, which we will review later). As such, they should be drafted in a way that signals the applicable party has the obligation to perform *after* the effective date of the agreement. Drafters commonly use "shall" or "will" to accomplish this small, yet important, task:

→ *Fitness Feet <u>will</u> pay Consultant $2,000 by wire transfer no later than seven days following the effective date of this Agreement.*

→ *Sporty Supply <u>shall</u> supply fitness trackers to Fitness Feet in accordance with Fitness Feet's purchase order.*

Whichever you choose (shall or will), the growing custom is to simply be consistent in your usage throughout the agreement. Although there are divergent interpretations of the word "shall,"[6] it would be difficult for a court to interpret the term (or "will") to mean anything other than signaling an obligation if it is the only word used to signal an obligation throughout an entire document. Varying the words used to indicate covenants runs the risk of introducing ambiguity with no tangible benefit. Most contract disputes are settled or resolved amicably, where bargaining power is dominant in determining the outcome, and the meaning of the words is never adjudicated. Additionally, in the rare instance your contract ends up in court, that court could find that using two different words ("shall" and "will") means that those words have different meanings. Make it easy on yourself and pick one and stick with it.

From a drafting standpoint, that means that if you are the initial drafter of an agreement, you can choose your preferred verb. However, if you are on the receiving end of a draft, then humble yourself to whichever approach the drafter chose. Although it can be difficult, sometimes lawyers have to set their own personal drafting preferences aside to get a deal done. Additionally, a lawyer risks looking like a jerk and wasting a client's time and money if their markup is full of nonsubstantive changes. You do not want to set a tone for a negotiation (and business relationship) that suggests trivial items will be controversial, which does not help you or the client. No client is impressed by lawyers wasting precious negotiation capital on inconsequential semantics (and they would rightfully be hesitant to pay a bill for those edits). More on that is presented in Chapter 7.

---

[6] Gutierrez de Martinez v. Lamagno, 505 U.S. 417 (1995), at n.9 ("Though 'shall' generally means 'must,' legal writers sometimes use, or misuse, 'shall' to mean 'should,' 'will,' or even 'may.'").

Exercise 2-3:

Look at the list of covenants you made for the Fitness Feet and Sporty Supply agreement in Exercise 2-2. Try drafting one sentence for each covenant that could be slotted into a contract, being consistent in your use of "shall" or "will." You may decide to combine two of the covenants you previously identified into one sentence.

Covenant 1:

_____

_____

Covenant 2:

_____

_____

Covenant 3:

_____

_____

Covenant 4:

_____

_____

Covenant 5:

_____

_____

Covenant 6 (if needed):

_____

_____

Remedies for Breaches of Covenants

As discussed earlier, covenants obligate a party to perform a particular act within the context of the relationship memorialized in the agreement. If a party breaches (i.e., fails to perform) a covenant, then the other side can turn to contract doctrine for the default remedies provided by the law.[7] Understanding the basic remedies associated with a

---

[7] Restatement (Second) of Contracts, § 1(e), 2 (Am. Law Inst.).

breach of a covenant will inform your drafting and negotiation and help you counsel your clients. For instance, you may find that the remedy available in the event of a breach of a covenant will not be enough to get your client comfortable, and you need to include additional protections (e.g., through an indemnity or uncapped liability exposure, both discussed later).

Generally speaking, a breach of a covenant excuses the other side's performance *if the breach is material*.[8] If the breach is not material, then a party can seek ordinary contract damages (such as the types taught in law school contracts classes—restitution, expectation damages, etc.), or specific performance.[9] In that case, the nonbreaching party is unlikely to be entitled to walk away from the contract, unless the agreement expressly allows for termination in the event of immaterial breaches.[10] In the absence of such language, a client should be counseled against relying on immaterial breaches as an excuse to disavow its own contractual obligations. This is important to remember when thinking through termination provisions and whether what is drafted or proposed will get your client out of the contract in the appropriate circumstances, without having to rely on arguments over whether a breach is sufficiently material.[11]

Licenses

There is one important set of contract provisions that are not drafted as future performance obligations, but are inherently covenants: licenses to intellectual property and other proprietary rights (copyrights, patents, trademarks, trade secrets, rights of publicity, etc.). For that reason, I include licenses in this section.

A license is, practically speaking (and except in rare instances that are beyond the scope of this book), the inverse side of a covenant. When a party (the "licensor") grants a license to intellectual property rights to another party, it is effectively promising that it will not sue the

---

[8] 13 JOSEPH M. PERILLO ET AL., CORBIN ON CONTRACTS, § 68.2 (rev. ed. 2009) ("Only if the effects of the breach are material is the legal duty of the other party suspended or discharged."). Be sure to check your state law to understand any variances from the general rule.

[9] Restatement (Second) of Contracts, § 346(a) (AM. LAW INST.) (1981).

[10] This may be accomplished by a termination provision that allows a party to terminate "for breach" (as opposed to "for material breach").

[11] One way of handling this is to deem breaches of particularly sensitive provisions to be "material breaches" under the contract. "For clarity, a breach of Section XX, YY, or ZZ will be deemed a material breach under this Agreement."

receiving party (the "licensee") for infringement when the licensee uses that intellectual property in accordance with the license scope. That promise to not file a claim in court is referred to as a "*covenant* not to sue." However, licenses are usually (but not always) drafted as the grant of affirmative rights, not a negative covenant preventing a party from filing a lawsuit.[12]

→ *Licensor grants Licensee a license to reproduce and distribute Licensee's book.*

You may notice that the license grant is drafted in the present tense and not as a future obligation. There is no "shall" or "will" to signal forthcoming performance. This is intentional. Licenses are drafted in the present tense so that the grant of rights is effectuated upon execution of the agreement.[13] However, any consideration provided by a party in exchange for the license grant remains framed as a future obligation:

→ *Licensor grants Licensee a license to Licensor's logo [present tense license grant]. In exchange for the license granted in this Agreement, Licensee will pay Licensor 15% of the revenues received by Licensee for sale of the products that bear the logo per month during the Term [future tense covenant].*

A license should only be drafted in the future tense in the rare case that the parties expressly intend to execute additional documentation to effectuate the license grant.[14] Drafting a license grant with "shall" or "will" ("Licensor shall grant Licensee a license") is, when governed by US law,[15] otherwise wrong, and a lawyer should be very clear with a client that more paperwork will be necessary to fully realize the intent of the contract if a present-tense license grant is not drafted. A present-tense grant is required even if the license is conditioned upon a future event, such as the creation of the work being licensed. For instance, if Fitness Feet hires a consultant to develop some software, but the consultant will

---

[12] There may be situations in which it makes more sense to draft an express negative covenant (not to sue) instead of an affirmative license, but those are beyond the scope of this book.

[13] The same is true for an assignment (i.e., transfer of ownership) of intellectual property rights. Drafters should also take care to not say "agree to assign" or "agree to license," which also signals something may need to happen in the future. The safest approach is a plain, present-tense statement. *See* Stanford University v. Roche Molecular Systems, Inc., 563 U.S. 776 (2011).

[14] *Id.*

[15] Other jurisdictions may take other approaches to the drafting of license grants.

retain ownership of the rights in that code, then Fitness Feet will need a broad license to that code once it has been created and delivered. The proper way to draft the license grant is as follows:

➔ *Upon delivery* of the work product, Consultant *grants* Fitness Feet a perpetual, irrevocable, nonexclusive, sublicensable license to reproduce, distribute, create derivative works of, perform, display, sublicense, and otherwise use the work product throughout the world.

The license is effective upon delivery of the work product, and no further documents memorializing the license grant are needed because of the present-tense grant (although the work product does not exist as of the date of the grant). If the license was drafted to say, "Upon delivery of the work product, Consultant will grant Fitness Feet a license," then the Consultant and Fitness Feet must take the additional step of effectuating that grant by signing another document upon delivery of the work product. That approach prejudices Fitness Feet because it creates additional hoops to jump through before Fitness Feet has the rights it needs to exploit the work product. The Consultant may not be interested in the extra paperwork, either. As such, a drafter should assume both parties intend for a present-tense grant unless expressly instructed otherwise.[16]

Another distinction between licenses and customary covenants is the remedies available. A license breach can give rise to different remedies than simple breaches of covenants because of the interplay between license grants and intellectual property law—intellectual property doctrine has its own set of remedies. If a license grant is breached, then the nonbreaching party may be able to recover damages calculated under intellectual property laws, in addition to contract damages, if available.[17] The intellectual property infringement damages are usually only available for breaches of the license grant and not any other terms. Breaches of contract provisions other than the license grant are analyzed under contract principles.

---

[16] As with all rules, there are exceptions. Some merger and acquisition agreements may use the "future grant" approach if there is a separate signing and closing to the acquisition. At closing, there will be many other documents signed, so adding an extra one that effectuates a license or other transfer of IP is not a burden. In license or other commercial agreements, however, there is usually not a "signing" and "closing" that necessitates additional paperwork.

[17] And notably, if an infringement claim is available, then (depending on the nature of the infringement) a prevailing party may be able to recover attorneys' fees.

> **Exercise 2-4:**
>
> Let's revisit the covenants you drafted for Fitness Feet and Sporty Supply in Exercise 2-3. Now, imagine Sporty Supply needs a license to Fitness Feet's logo so that it can put Fitness Feet branding on the trackers it is manufacturing. How will you draft the license?
>
> _____
>
> _____
>
> _____

Risk-Shifting Provisions

In General

Risk-shifting provisions are clauses whose primary functions are to allocate risk between the parties. These consist primarily of representations and warranties, indemnification, and the limitations on liability. The "risk" that is being shifted between the parties is the liability that may arise from nonperformance of the agreement, violations of law, and/or harm caused to third parties as a result of the parties' relationship. Clients may (and often do) refer to these terms as the "legal sections," which should suggest to any lawyer that their advice will be critical for these provisions. In many cases, an attorney's greatest value-add will be advice on how to draft and negotiate these terms, which are typically beyond the scope of the "business deal" that the client's business team has agreed to with their counterparts.

We will revisit Fitness Feet's deal with Sporty Supply soon, but note for now how Casey's email to you in Exercise 2-2 about the deal did not say anything about indemnification or liability caps. That is to be expected, especially when dealing with a nonlawyer. Clients will look to you to suggest what is reasonable, necessary, or customary in the given industry in terms of risk allocation and to convey that information back to them. Our job, as attorneys, is to not only draft and negotiate the language but to also inform our clients _why_ we might be recommending a particular position, what the remedy is for a breach, and if (and where) there is wiggle room to negotiate. After all, it is the client's money and liability that are on the line, not ours. The client should understand how it might be spent. Let's dig in.

Representations and Warranties

A representation is a statement of fact that the recipient has relied on in entering into the contract,[18] usually relating to the state or condition of a party or its business (including its operations, products, and services). By definition, then, it cannot be made about the future—no one can reasonably rely on something that has not yet occurred. Therefore, technically speaking, the representation should only be made as to the past or the present state of affairs. For example,

→ *Fitness Feet represents that the development and manufacturing of its fitness trackers, as currently conducted, do not infringe any third party's patents.*

→ *Consultant represents that Consultant has all licenses and permits necessary to perform services for Fitness Feet.*

→ *Fitness Feet represents that it is a corporation organized under Delaware law.*

And yet, as we will soon see, future statements are often included within the scope of a representation. Keep in mind for now, though, that the definition of a representation requires that it only relate to the past or present.

Representations are rarely made without their partner in crime, warranties ("Company represents *and warrants* that . . ."). Warranties are promises made about the past, present, *or future*, but like representations, they are typically made about the condition or state of an entity or item.[19] Neither representations nor warranties are covenants. They are not promises to perform. Rather, they are statements of attributes that an entity or item will have (in the case of warranties) or already has (in the case of either representations or warranties). A party may make representations and warranties as to certain certifications it has obtained, its authority to do business in a particular jurisdiction, its compliance with laws and the legality of its business practices, the safety and viability of its products, and more.

If a representation is not true, then a "misrepresentation" has been made, and an action may be brought in tort, in some cases (e.g., if the misrepresentation was fraudulent), as well as contract, for damages.[20]

---

[18] 7 JOSEPH M. PERILLO ET AL., CORBIN ON CONTRACTS, § 28.15 (rev. ed. 2009); Restatement (Second) of Contracts, § 164(d) (AM. LAW INST.) (1981).

[19] As an aside, warranties may also refer to separate documents, such as a limited warranty for consumer products that describes the repair and/or replacement process for faulty consumer goods. The drafting of stand-alone product warranties is largely governed by applicable federal and state laws.

[20] 7 JOSEPH M. PERILLO ET AL., CORBIN ON CONTRACTS, § 28.23 (rev. ed. 2009).

In contrast to representations, a breach of a warranty will solely give rise to damages determined under contract law principles (similar to covenants).

In bilateral contracts (which include commercial business contracts, as well as merger, asset, or other acquisition agreements), representations and warranties are *almost always* drafted together, notwithstanding the fact that they are legally distinct concepts that can give rise to different sets of remedies.

➜ *Company represents and warrants that it will comply and has complied with all laws applicable to its performance under this agreement.*

As noted earlier, parties use representations and warranties (collectively) to give and receive assurances about the state of their business and, in many circumstances, how they will conduct their business and perform under an agreement. Although the typical drafting approach muddies the distinction between representations and warranties, there are benefits to this approach that outweigh the downsides of the technical inaccuracy of a forward-looking representation. Namely, by getting a representation and warranty as to a certain fact, a party maximizes its potential damages and affords that party the most options for seeking a remedy if the statement turns out to be untrue. From a more practical standpoint, drafters like to pair the two in the interest of efficiency. The alternative would be to draft two sections that largely overlap.

A standard representations and warranties section in a simple business contract might look like this:

➜ *Company A represents and warrants to Company B that (a) the person executing this Agreement on its behalf has the authority to do so, (b) Company A's software products do not infringe any third party's intellectual property rights, and (c) Company A will comply with all applicable laws in the performance of this Agreement.*

Note that some of the representations and warranties mentioned earlier may also relate to covenants. A drafter (and client) may want assurances as to certain conditions existing as of the effective date (via representations and warranties) as well as promises to take actions to maintain or change those conditions during the term of the agreement (via a covenant).

➜ *Covenant: Company A's software products will not infringe any third party's intellectual property rights.*
Representation and Warranty: Company A's software products do not infringe any third party's intellectual property rights.

→ *Covenant: Consultant will develop and deliver software code.*
   Representation and Warranty: Consultant represents and warrants that
   the software deliverables will be free from viruses.

→ *Covenant: Fitness Feet will repair any wearable fitness tracker that has a*
   material defect.
   Representation and Warranty: Fitness Feet represents and warrants that
   its fitness trackers are free from any material defects for 12 months from
   the date of purchase.

Take the last example. A recipient of the representation and warranty may have a claim against Fitness Feet for breach of contract (i.e., the warranty) if it buys a tracker that has a material defect during the year following the purchase of the tracker. That recipient would also have a claim under tort law if it could be proven that a fraudulent misrepresentation was also made. Separately, under the contract, Fitness Feet is required to repair that tracker. Fortunately, if Fitness Feet fixes the tracker, then the buyer is unlikely to also want to sue Fitness Feet for damages—presumably all the buyer cares about is having a functioning tracker. So, taking this provision a step further, an astute drafter will link the two concepts together by making the repair covenant the buyer's sole remedy for a breach of the warranty, and eliminate the ability for the recipient to be able to sue for breach of contract.

→ *Fitness Feet represents and warrants that its fitness trackers are free from*
   any material defects for 12 months from the date of purchase. As Buyer's
   sole remedy for a breach of the immediately preceding representation and
   warranty, Fitness Feet will repair any wearable fitness tracker that has a
   material defect and is reported to Fitness Feet within 12 months from the
   date of purchase.

A similar approach can be taken with respect to the Consultant and its software code:

→ *Consultant will develop and deliver software code. Consultant represents*
   and warrants that such software code will be free from viruses. As Com-
   pany's sole remedy for a breach of the immediately foregoing representation
   and warranty, Consultant will develop and deliver revised virus-free soft-
   ware code with the same functionality and features as originally developed
   and delivered.

When drafting representations and warranties (and discussing with your client whether to seek certain representations and warranties), consider what assurances you need from the other side as a prerequisite to getting the deal done. This exercise should not be taken as an opportunity to throw in the kitchen sink. Part of being thoughtful about how the representations and warranties that are worth seeking is considering the benefit gained. Said differently, what sort of guarantees do you *need* about the state of the other side's business to be comfortable entering into the deal, and what sort of guarantees do you *want* but could negotiate away if needed? In a business contract context, I might think about the following:

1. *Compliance with any laws or regulations that are specific to the other side's business.* For example, if the other side sends unsolicited text messages as part of its service, a representation and warranty that that service complies with the Telephone Consumer Protection Act, which regulates the sending of certain promotional text messages, is a good start. Similarly, there is a growing number of laws around the world regulating how companies can use individuals' personal information with serious penalties for noncompliance. If a deal involves the exchange of personal information, I'll want to think about which of those laws apply (if any) and seek some assurances about compliance.

2. *Infringement of intellectual property rights.* The infringement (or lack thereof) of intellectual property rights is typically addressed in its own representation and warranty. A representation and warranty about noninfringement of intellectual property rights will typically also include a catchall for any other "proprietary rights," which would include rights of privacy and publicity, as well as moral rights (which are recognized in many countries around the world, but not the United States).

3. *Corporate organization and authority.* You will commonly see (and want to receive) representations and warranties about a company's lawful organization and its authority to do business. This assures you, among other things, that there is a legal entity on the other side of the contract in the event you need to bring a lawsuit or other action.

4. *No conflicting arrangements.* You may also want assurances in the agreement that the other side does not have any outstanding contractual obligations that would prevent it from entering into the agreement with you. If the other side has agreed to an exclusive arrangement that your relationship with the other side would violate, for instance, asking for a representation and warranty will ferret out that information before the deal is signed.

There are ample other avenues to consider when working in other contexts. For example, if you are drafting an agreement to acquire another company, you will be looking for representations and warranties related to current litigation, taxes, export controls, issuances of stock or other equity, and executive compensation.

After deciding which concepts to cover in your representations and warranties, a choice must be made as to how narrow or broad to make the language. Consider the difference between these two examples:

→ *Example 1: Licensor represents and warrants that the Licensed Intellectual Property does not infringe any US patents or copyrights.*

→ *Example 2: Licensor represents and warrants that the Licensed Intellectual Property does not infringe any third party's intellectual or proprietary rights, anywhere throughout the world.*

Clearly, if you represent the Licensor, Example 1 benefits you; if you are the Licensee, Example 2 is more favorable. Both could be reasonable, depending on the circumstances of the deal. There are several other ways to construct this representation and warranty and stay on the spectrum of reasonableness. Knowing where you are on that spectrum is helpful, as there is typically some room to move over the course of a negotiation, and you will need to work with your client to figure out the bounds of their own risk tolerance, as well as inform them where those bounds may lie in the greater market based on your experience.

Exercise 2-5:

Let's revisit Fitness Feet's agreement with Sporty Supply for the manufacture and supply of fitness trackers (see Exercises 2-3 and 2-4). Given that Sporty Supply is going to be on the hook for supplying Fitness Feet with the product on which its entire business is based and that Fitness Feet is going to turn around and sell that product to consumers, can you come up with three to four representations and warranties that Fitness Feet might seek from Sporty Supply?

Representation and Warranty #1:

_____

_____

Representation and Warranty #2:

_____

_____

> Representation and Warranty #3:
>
> _____
>
> _____
>
> Representation and Warranty #4:
>
> _____
>
> _____

Indemnification

If there is one legal concept that plays a starring role in almost every private sector lawyer's practice (transactional or litigation), it is indemnification. And yet, I worked with many associates who confessed to having left law school without ever hearing the term, much less understanding what it means. Indemnification is a rarely discussed principle in academia but one of the most significant in practice. Clients appreciate when their lawyers take the time to educate them on these hyperlegal concepts and why they matter. Without this knowledge, they cannot really provide you, as the attorney, meaningful input on what makes business sense for them in terms of risk allocation.

Indemnification is the means by which a client will seek recourse for certain claims. The importance of appropriately allocating liability for indemnification cannot be overstated, nor can the importance of making sure your client understands what an indemnity is and the risk it is taking on—so _you_ better understand. In fact, there were _many_ times over the course of my career where the _only_ section of a contract that a cost-sensitive client would ask me to review was the indemnity. This is because to nonlawyers, indemnification can appear to be the most "legal" in nature, given the use of unfamiliar terminology, and therefore is the "scariest" to edit without counsel's direction. As such, it is important to get it right. Relatedly, I have seen a lot of lawyers who never seek their clients' feedback on indemnification provisions because it requires explaining a complicated legal concept. That approach can create a real problem down the road if the indemnity is actually triggered. Clients need to know going into the deal what they are signing up for and how much of their money is on the line in certain circumstances. They cannot be learning that information for the first time when a problem arises. You might also be surprised to find out where their comfort level is for indemnification obligations.

Indemnification is often easier to understand when framed as being similar to an insurance policy against certain claims. *Insurance* is a near-universally understood concept in the business world and so the analogy is accessible to most.[21] Like insurance, indemnification is a means to guarantee that a party is made whole (or partially whole) when certain, negotiated-for harms occur. There are two groups of situations for which indemnity is usually allocated: first-party claims and third-party claims.

First-Party Claims

First-party claims are claims between the two parties to the contract: One party commits a harm against the other party, and the contract requires the first party to indemnify the other for the losses or other damages resulting from the harm. This is distinct from contract damages resulting from the breach. There could realistically be an indemnifiable claim but no breach of contract.

For example, a home construction contract might provide that a contractor will indemnify the homeowner if any of the contractor's subcontractors acted negligently. That same contract may not have a correlating covenant pursuant to which the contractor affirmatively promises that its subcontractors will not act negligently. If a plumber then negligently drops a hammer on a water pipe in the home, causing it to burst open and flood the basement of the home, then the contractor's indemnification obligation would likely kick in. Without a covenant about subcontractors' negligence, the homeowner probably would not have a separate breach of contract claim against the contractor, so the homeowner would rely exclusively on the indemnity for some recourse. The indemnification clause might look like this:

→ *Contractor will indemnify Homeowner for all losses, liabilities, damages, fees, expenses, penalties, and other liabilities incurred as a result of any Subcontractors' negligent acts on the premises.*

Because of the indemnity clause, the Contractor will likely have to pay to clean up the water mess and fix the pipe—but it will not have to separately defend itself from a breach of contract lawsuit in court.

---

[21] One of the main differences between actual insurance and indemnification, though, is that you can be fairly certain your insurance company will have the funds to pay out your policy if the need arises. You cannot always be certain your contractual counterparty will be solvent enough to back up their indemnity, and if you think the counterparty may be "judgment proof," then you should flag that for your client.

There are, however, situations in which a particular harm gives rise to an indemnification obligation and a breach of contract claim. In the plumbing situation, if the contract did, in fact, require the Contractor to ensure its subcontractors do not act negligently, then the homeowner could also sue the contractor for a breach of contract. This creates a messy reality, though, that illustrates why these "direct" indemnification obligations are uncommon in business scenarios.

A typical indemnification provision requires the indemnifying party to cover any "liabilities, losses, fees, penalties, expenses," and other damages that the indemnified party incurs as a result of the harm caused by the indemnifying party. If the indemnified party is suing the indemnifying party for breach of contract, then the expenses that indemnified party sustains as part of the harm include all of the costs to take the other party to court for the contract claim. In other words, the indemnifying party (the Contractor in our example) will end up paying the other party (the homeowner) the costs of suing itself. The homeowner is thus incentivized to bring the breach of contract claim, because it will have its costs covered. It is (at least in part) for this reason that indemnification for first-party claims is unusual in business contracts. Nobody wants to foot the bill for somebody else to sue them.

Third-Party Claims

Indemnification provisions that require a party to indemnify the other in the event a third party brings a claim against the indemnified party are much more common (and appropriate) in commercial relationships. These are situations in which a third party (which can be a private actor, i.e., other company or individual, or government authority/agency) asserts an action against, or is harmed by, one party to the contract as a result of the other party's actions. Take a look at these common examples:

➜ *Party A will indemnify and defend Party B from and against any and all third-party claims, suits, allegations, losses, fees, penalties, costs, and expenses arising from or related to (a) Party A's negligence or willful misconduct in performing this Agreement, (b) the work product Party A delivers to Party B when used by Party B as intended by this Agreement, and (c) Party A's violation or alleged violation of any law, rule, or regulation.*

➜ *Party A will indemnify and defend Party B against all third-party claims, suits, allegations, costs, fees, penalties, losses, and expenses incurred as a result of an allegation that Party A's intellectual property, as licensed to Party B and used as permitted under this Agreement, infringes a third party's proprietary rights.*

→ *Party A will indemnify and defend Party B against all costs, fees, pen-alties, losses, and expenses incurred as a result of a finally adjudicated or settled claim or lawsuit brought by a third party alleging that Party A failed to comply with all applicable laws (including privacy laws) in its performance of this Agreement.*

Constructing an Indemnification Provision

After determining whether you are going to seek or receive indemnifi-cation for first- or third-party claims, consider how the indemnification obligation will be triggered: (1) the nature of the claim (adjudicated or alleged) that will give rise to indemnification; (2) the relation of the claim to the harmful act (arising under, related to, or as a result of); and (3) the substance of the indemnifiable claims. These are discussed next.

The first two buckets relate to how the indemnification is triggered. There are different ways that you can draft these triggers for an indem-nification obligation: allegations of claims, adjudicated claims, claims directly arising from conduct, or claims related to conduct. I do not exaggerate when I say the options are almost endless and often chosen in an arbitrary manner. I encourage you to think carefully about what sort of trigger is best for your client in the given situation. There is a big difference between an indemnification triggered only by a fully adjudi-cated claim (which requires there be a lawsuit and a final decision on that lawsuit, either by settlement or judicial decision) and a claim that is alleged (e.g., filed in court or the subject of a cease-and-desist let-ter) but not adjudicated. Indemnity obligations that are triggered only by adjudicated claims may benefit your client (if it is the indemnifying party) in a situation where a third-party claim against the other party is withdrawn or never filed in court, but that party has still incurred costs. But if your client is the one benefiting from indemnification, then you might be out of luck if the claim is never judicially resolved.

Similarly, think about the differences between provisions that pro-vide for indemnification from claims that "arise out of" or "result from" certain conduct versus claims that simply "relate to" that conduct.

→ *Party A will indemnify and defend Party B from and against any and all third-party claims, suits, allegations, losses, fees, penalties, costs, and expenses arising out of Party A's negligence or willful misconduct in per-forming this Agreement.*

→ *Party A will indemnify and defend Party B from and against any and all third-party claims, suits, allegations, losses, fees, penalties, costs, and expenses relating to Party A's negligence or willful misconduct in perform-ing this Agreement.*

In the first example ("arising out of"), the negligence or willful misconduct must have some causal relation to the claim.[22] This is in contrast to the second example ("relating to"), where the claim need not be caused by the negligence or willful misconduct; there must be a nexus between the claim and the negligence.[23] As you may have seen in the examples in the "Third-Party Claims" section, some drafters go ahead and include both "arising from" and "relating to" to ensure the broadest possible coverage, although "relating to" is so broad, it likely encompasses anything that also "arises out of" the same circumstances.

The last, and most substantive, component of an indemnification provision includes the claims for which you are receiving or giving indemnity. In a perfect world, your client would be indemnified for any conceivable (or even inconceivable) claim brought against them that relates, directly or indirectly, to the contract and is remotely related to the counterparty's actions. But business lawyers don't operate in ideal worlds—they operate in reality. Being pragmatic about which claims you are seeking indemnification for can pay dividends over the course of a negotiation. This is particularly true because your client will look to you to lead the advocacy efforts for this part of the agreement, and appearing uncompromising because you refuse to drop an overly broad indemnity position does not benefit you (or your reputation) or your client.

Drafting Guidelines

To guide your drafting of indemnities, following are the key questions to ask yourself when thinking about the provisions and some more examples to aid your thinking. There are no bright lines to apply. Rather, each of the following questions should be considered in light of your client's leverage, their ability to pay for the applicable claim (and as a corollary, the other side's ability to pay), and which party is in the better position to avoid the harm contemplated (and therefore should be the indemnifying party for that harm).

1. What *plausible* claims might a third party bring against your client relating to the deal?

Think about realistic risks inherent in entering into the deal with the particular counterparty (the all-too-useful "what might go wrong" line of thinking). Consider the industry the parties operate in, any

---

[22] *See, e.g.*, Coregis Ins. Co. v. Am. Health Found., 241 F. 3d 123, 128 (2d Cir. 2001) (determining that "arising out of" requires some "causal relationship").

[23] *See, e.g.*, *id.* (finding that "'related to' is typically defined more broadly [than 'arising out of'] and is not necessarily tied to the concept of a causal connection").

applicable legal regimes, and the nature of the parties' products and services. Keeping a chart like the following might prove helpful. I've filled it out for basic commercial agreements, but you can customize it for your practice area and the common risks you see.

Circumstance/Risk	Indemnifiable Claims
Individuals' personal information is being transferred or used (or other privacy concerns)	Violation of applicable privacy legislation throughout the world (or where relevant)
One party is using the other party's intellectual property	Licensor party to indemnify licensee party for intellectual property infringement claims
Contract involves sale or use of physical/tangible goods (other party is *not* a consumer)	Consider product liability, personal injury, negligence, willful misconduct

To see how you might ascertain what claims you should seek indemnity for in practice, let's examine Fitness Feet and Sporty Supply. Fitness Feet has mentioned to you that they believe Sporty Supply will make a great tracker for them, but they are concerned about what might happen if the trackers malfunction and do not work as intended after being sold to consumers. You have also expressed your concerns to Fitness Feet about potential class action litigation, which can be very expensive if a lot of consumers band together in one lawsuit. Therefore, it would be reasonable for you, on behalf of Fitness Feet, to ask for indemnification from product liability claims arising out of Fitness Feet's and its customers' use of the tracker as it is intended to be used.

   2. What *plausible* claims might be brought against the other party that would be reasonable for your client to be on the hook for?

As a general rule, it is reasonable to give indemnification for two buckets of claims: those which, if brought, would be primarily (or exclusively) your client's fault, and those for which your client can more easily (than the other side) obtain insurance. You might not include all of these claims in your initial draft (as we discuss later), but it is good practice for you to think about the different claims in advance and discuss with your client.

   In drafting Fitness Feet's agreement with Sporty Supply, Fitness Feet is going to grant Sporty Supply a license to use Fitness Feet's patents and trade secrets so that Sporty Supply can effectively manufacture the trackers to Fitness Feet's specifications and design. Sporty Supply would be reasonable in asking Fitness Feet to indemnify Sporty Supply for claims brought by a third party alleging that Fitness Feet's intellectual property infringes that third party's intellectual property. Litigation, and particularly patent and trade secrets litigation, is very expensive and time consuming, and as between Fitness Feet and Sporty Supply, it is fair for Fitness Feet to insure Sporty Supply for claims relating to Fitness Feet's intellectual property portfolio. Sporty Supply is simply exercising the rights being granted to it in order to provide a service.

It would be less fair for Sporty Supply to ask Fitness Feet to indemnify Sporty Supply if Sporty Supply uses the licensed intellectual property in a manner beyond the scope of the license grant or otherwise in breach of the agreement. Sporty Supply should be on the hook for its unauthorized conduct. Fitness Feet also should not indemnify for any claims arising out of Sporty Supply's own technology used for the manufacture of or incorporated into the trackers. Be sure that when you draft your indemnification provision, you are not unintentionally including these less reasonable claims.

3. How broad or narrow should the "trigger" (arising out of, related to, directly resulting from) be?

This depends in large part on the leverage the client has as well as how broad the indemnifiable claims are. If you have a broad set of indemnifiable claims, you may be able to live with a narrower trigger.

Assume that Sporty Supply, while an established company, does not have a lot of consumers and needs this deal with Fitness Feet as much as Fitness Feet needs a good manufacturer, so the leverage is about equal. You will almost certainly want an indemnity for product liability claims, but you can probably live with a narrow trigger ("as a result of") and a broad set of claims ("*any* claim of a defect"), since Sporty Supply will have control over the manufacturing process, and any defects will likely be the company's fault.

As for the intellectual property infringement indemnification that Fitness Feet is giving Sporty Supply, you, as Fitness Feet's lawyer, will want to keep both the trigger and the claims as narrow as possible (but you might give a bit on one of those components to get the deal done).

4. How much work and time will your client need to put in to get the benefit of the indemnity it has negotiated for? Will it need to wait for a breach to be proven? Will it have to go to court to prove any particular event has happened?

For a product liability claim, you will probably want to ensure some coverage as soon as the claim is filed. You do not want to have to wait for a claim to be adjudicated before your client can recover anything, particularly if a class action lawsuit is possible. The same is true for most other cases, but in other contexts (for claims that are less expensive, less time consuming, and less business critical), you might be able to settle for fully adjudicated.

As you are probably starting to see, negotiating and drafting an indemnification provision is more of an art than a science. There are very few rules, and the path to a final draft is littered with gives and takes that are determined in large part by leverage and reasonableness, each of which is unique to the deal at hand.

Claims Arising from a Breach

With that context about how to think about the claims that the indemnification provision should cover, let's revisit the all-too-common practice of asking for indemnity for any claims relating to (or arising out of) a "breach of the representations and warranties" in (or, in some cases, all terms of) the agreement, instead of identifying more specific claims, which may or may not relate to the representations and warranties.

While indemnities for a breach of the representations and warranties often show up in business contracts, they originate from the mergers and acquisitions (M&A) context. The distinction between the two worlds is critical here. In a business contract, as we know, a breach of representations and warranties facilitates a claim for damages under contract (and potentially tort) law. Technically speaking, the same is true in a merger agreement; however, practically speaking, an acquirer is extremely unlikely to sue a company it just acquired for damages. Instead, it will just want the acquired company to cover its losses, and there are numerous contractual mechanisms that can be engaged to facilitate that coverage. As such, in M&A, the indemnity is the most logical recourse (and the most realistic recourse) for a claim for a breach of representations and warranties.

By way of example, if there is a breach of the representation and warranty that an acquired company makes assuring the acquirer that the operation of its business has not infringed any third party's intellectual property rights, then the acquired company should indemnify the acquirer for any associated losses (such as having to defend an infringement lawsuit or replacing the infringing intellectual property with non-infringing intellectual property). But, the acquirer has no incentive to sue its own subsidiary for contract damages—all of the money comes out of the same corporate family. As such, it relies on the indemnity (which usually comes out of a set-aside bucket of money) to be made whole. Compare that to a business deal, however, where the parties are not related and can rely on lawsuits and damages claims to solve for breaches of representations and warranties.

A blanket indemnity for all breaches of the representations and warranties is really only appropriate in the rare business deal where it truly makes sense for a party to indemnify the other for losses related to a breach of *each and every* representation and warranty. Breaches of most representations and warranties are really unlikely to give rise to a claim worthy of indemnification. As an example, a party commonly represents and warrants that it is validly organized under the laws of a particular state. If that is not true, it is extremely doubtful that a third party will sue the recipient of that representation and warranty in a way that would cause losses worth the negotiation of the indemnity. Put more concretely, if Sporty Supply represented and warranted it was validly organized under Delaware law, and it turns out that representation and warranty was false, the chances of Fitness Feet being sued as a result are infinitesimal. As a result, it is not really pragmatic to ask for an indemnity for a breach of that representation and warranty—and I'm not sure you could explain to your client why you would. So, be judicious in your use of indemnification to solve for breaches of all representations and warranties.

In Practice

Let's review the Sporty Supply and Fitness Feet deal a bit more to see how this plays out in practice. Ashley sends you a precedent contract as a basis to use for the deal. The precedent has the following provisions:

➔ *11.2. <u>Supplier's Representations and Warranties</u>. Supplier represents and warrants to Company that (a) it is duly organized under the laws of Delaware, (b) the person executing this Agreement on Supplier's behalf has the authority to do so, (c) Supplier complies with all applicable laws in the operation of its business, and (d) Supplier's products and services do not infringe any third party's intellectual property rights.*

. . .

➔ *12.2. <u>Supplier's Indemnification</u>. Supplier will indemnify and defend Company from any and all third-party claims, suits, allegations, costs, fees, penalties, losses, and expenses arising out of or related to Supplier's breach of its representations and warranties in this Agreement.*

You walk into Ashley's office to ask some questions.

"Thanks for the precedent. I was taking a look and thinking about different approaches to take for Fitness Feet and have a couple of questions. First, in the precedent, the indemnification is for a breach of all the reps and warranties. What should I tell Fitness Feet if they ask why they would want an indemnity for a breach of the 'corporate authority'[24] reps. Is that really realistic?"

Ashley stammers a bit before answering. "Uh, it's probably a nonissue. It's unlikely to happen; that's just how these things are written." If you were a client, would you be satisfied with that answer? Particularly if you are paying several hundred dollars an hour for legal advice? I wouldn't be.

You make a mental note to be more precise in your draft about only asking for an indemnity for claims that are actually realistic before asking your second question. You know that in a commercial deal, indemnity is not the only recourse for a breach of representations and warranties. The parties can still sue each other, so Fitness Feet will not be left without a remedy if you ultimately narrow the indemnity scope a bit.

"When it says that Supplier will indemnify Company for claims arising out of a 'breach,' who determines whether a breach occurs? Would we have to wait for a claim to be adjudicated by a court before seeking indemnity? That seems bad for us."

Ashley agrees that is what it sounds like, and both of you are correct. "Breach" is a legal term and is only deemed to have occurred when a party does not perform under the contract without a "legal excuse."[25] As a result, when explaining to any client what it means for an indemnification obligation to be tied to a breach of the contract, it would be prudent to err on the side of explaining that the obligation may not kick in until after a court has determined a breach occurred. Only courts are equipped to adjudicate "legal excuses," adding an obstacle to recovery under the indemnity.

Exercise 2-6:

Now that we know that the precedent Ashley provided you is insufficient in terms of indemnification provisions, consider the four guidelines described in the "Drafting Guidelines" section and think about what sorts of liabilities might be implicated in doing a deal with a manufacturer (assume that Sporty Supply is a US company and will be supplying the trackers from a US facility) and would be reasonable to seek indemnification for.

Indemnifiable Claim #1:

---

[24] The corporate authority representations and warranties are those relating to a party's authority under corporate laws to operate and conduct business. In this case, they would be (a) and (b) in Section 11.2.

[25] AM. JUR. 2D *Contracts* § 669 (1998).

Indemnifiable Claim #2:

_____

Indemnifiable Claim #3:

_____

Limitations of Liability

The last of the risk-shifting provisions is the limitations of liability. While certain parts of the limitations of liability are not often negotiated, others are and have a significant effect on a client's risk profile under the agreement.

The limitations of liability refer to terms that seek to limit a party's risk under a contract for all or some claims brought by the other party (which can include claims for indemnification). These provisions generally consist of two components: a "cap" on direct (monetary) damages and a disclaimer of indirect damages, each of which we review in turn.

Damages Cap

The cap on direct damages limits how much each party can collect from the other in the event of a claim between the parties that relates to or is brought under the contract (i.e., a breach of a contract claim). There are two aspects to consider when drafting this provision: The value of the cap and which claims are covered under the cap.

As a general rule, it is customary to try and tie the liability cap to the value of the contract in an arm's-length commercial deal. A common approach is to make the cap equal to the fees paid or payable under the contract in a particular time period. If one party is paying recurring (whether fixed or variable) fees to another party, the value of those fees over the twelve or twenty-four months prior to the event giving rise to liability is a reasonable cap.

→ *IN NO EVENT WILL A PARTY'S LIABILITY FOR MONETARY DAMAGES UNDER THIS AGREEMENT EXCEED THE FEES PAID OR PAYABLE BY THAT PARTY IN THE 12 MONTHS PRIOR TO THE EVENT GIVING RISE TO THE CLAIM.*

Similarly, if there is a single value attributable to the contract (such as a one-time license fee), the cap might reflect that value.

→ *IN NO EVENT WILL EITHER PARTY'S LIABILITY FOR MONE-*
   TARY DAMAGES UNDER THIS AGREEMENT EXCEED THE
   LICENSE FEE PAYABLE UNDER SECTION 3.1.

In cases where the value of the contract cannot easily be quantified
in dollars, the parties may try to come up with a flat figure that seems
defensible and would provide some certainty. Negotiations over these
flat amounts can become arbitrary, however, so be mindful about the
actual impact on the client's business a claim brought for the maximum allowed amount will have. A client who can stomach a $1,000,000
expense might not feel the same way about $10,000,000 (and "adding a
zero" is not an uncommon negotiation tactic). If a flat figure is in play,
then consider asking your client whether it has an insurance policy that
would likely cover claims subject to the cap, and if so, what the deductible is for those policies. Ensuring the cap equals the deductible is a
thoughtful way of limiting what a client might have to pay out of pocket.

Exercise 2-7:

Recall that Fitness Feet will pay Sporty Supply $10 per tracker in the manufacturing
deal. What might you propose for a liability cap?

_____

_____

The claims to be covered by the liability cap should absolutely
include claims for breach of contract—after all, the mostly likely claim
to be brought under a contract is for breach of that contract. Additionally, the cap should apply to tort claims. It is easy to forget that tort
claims can relate to contract claims, but recall from earlier that a breach
of a representation (a "misrepresentation") technically gives rise to a
claim for damages in tort law, not contract law. If you do not exclude
tort claims from the cap, then you have potentially created an end run
around the liability cap for breaches of the representations (but not the
warranties). You will also often see a parenthetical signifying that negligence is included within tort claims for purposes of the cap:

→ *TO THE FULLEST EXTENT PERMITTED BY LAW, THE AGGRE-*
   GATE LIABILITY OF EITHER PARTY FOR ALL CLAIMS ARISING
   OUT OF THIS AGREEMENT, WHETHER BASED IN CONTRACT
   OR <u>*TORT (INCLUDING NEGLIGENCE)*</u>*, WILL NOT EXCEED THE*

AMOUNT OF THE FEES THAT WERE PAID OR ARE PAYABLE IN THE 12 MONTHS PRECEDING THE EVENT GIVING RISE TO THE CLAIM.

Some courts (particularly in California) have held that a party will not be released from claims for negligence unless the agreement is "clear, explicit, and comprehensible."[26] As a result, it would be prudent for drafters to err on the side of caution and be extra clear that when capping liability for tort, they also mean negligence. In determining whether it makes sense to include negligence claims within the cap, think about the likelihood of a negligence claim arising from your contract and which party is most likely to be in a position to act negligently.

Disclaimer of Indirect Damages

The second component of the limitation of liability is the disclaimer of indirect damages. This provision is where your familiarity with consequential damages from law school will come in handy. In the business agreement context, parties typically agree to exclude all liability for indirect damages, which usually includes consequential damages, for certain claims. They do this because neither party wants to open itself up to unlimited liability. Even though consequential damages must be "foreseeable," they can still be well beyond a reasonable amount each party is willing to pay to cover the impact of a breach. Except in cases where there is unusually disparate leverage, this provision is almost always made mutual and does not vary much from agreement to agreement. In representing hundreds of companies over several years, I negotiated the substantive text of the disclaimer only a handful of times (exclusions from the disclaimer are a different story). Where one side has more leverage, it is typically manipulated through exclusions from the cap and disclaimer, discussed next.

Exclusions from the Cap and Disclaimer of Indirect Damages

The most important aspect of drafting the limitation of liability—and the part that does get negotiated—is the exclusions. There are almost always certain claims that one or both parties believe should not be subject to the cap or included in the indirect damages disclaimer (in other words, the maximum potential recovery for those claims should be unlimited).

---

[26] Ferrell v. S. Nev. Off-Road Enthusiasts, 147 Cal. App. 3d 309, 318 (Cal Ct. App. 1983); *see also* Hohe v. San Diego Unified Sch. Dist., 224 Cal. App. 3d 1559 (Cal. Ct. App. 1990).

A classic and common example of an exclusion from the limitation of liability is any obligation payable under the indemnification provision. Given that the purpose of an indemnity is to make a party *whole* in the event of certain harms, subsequently capping that means of recourse guts the intent of the indemnity provision—and it is important for your client to understand this rationale when you are pushing to exclude your hard-fought indemnification wins. As such, the indemnification provision should always be considered in tandem with the limitation of liability to ensure your intent is carried through. Similarly, an increasing number of parties are seeking to carve out privacy and data security obligations from the limitations on liability because of the enhanced scrutiny on cybersecurity and potential for claims of data breaches and resulting harms.

If you are not winning your negotiation to keep certain claims uncapped, an alternative approach (albeit one to be used sparingly) is to agree to a separate, much larger cap on those claims. Again, this cap could also be tied to a party's insurance policies so that the party is not out-of-pocket more than the amount of the deductible. When discussing with your client what claims to exclude, you will need to think about which claims warrant more than what is effectively a partial or entire refund (assuming your cap is tied to the fees paid under the agreement) and which claims could result in damages that are too unpredictable to justify including in the cap.

Drafting the Limitation of Liability

As you have already seen in the previous examples, both parts of the limitation of liability section are typically drafted in all caps. This custom is likely a remnant from the Uniform Commercial Code (UCC), which requires that disclaimers or modifications of warranties be conspicuous.[27] Although the UCC may not apply to your contract, and the limitation of liability is not strictly a disclaimer or modification of warranty, widespread practice is to keep these provisions in all caps, and because there is no harm in doing so, keeping with custom in this case is fair.

→ *EXCEPT WITH RESPECT TO A PARTY'S INDEMNIFICATION OBLIGATIONS UNDER THIS AGREEMENT, (A) NEITHER PARTY WILL BE LIABLE TO THE OTHER PARTY FOR DIRECT DAMAGES*

---

[27] *See* U.C.C. § 2-316. Some commentators note that "conspicuous," even under the U.C.C., does not require all caps, and they would prefer to not be "yelled at" by their contracts. *See* Lily Hay Newman, *Why Are the Terms of Service Agreements We Never Read in All Caps?* SLATE (Dec. 23, 2015), https://slate.com/technology/2015/12/why-do-legal-documents-like-terms-of-service-agreements-often-include-all-caps.html.

IN EXCESS OF THE FEES PAID BY PARTY A TO PARTY B UNDER THIS AGREEMENT IN THE 12 MONTHS PRIOR TO THE EVENT GIVING RISE TO THE CLAIM, AND (B) NEITHER PARTY WILL BE LIABLE TO THE OTHER FOR ANY INDIRECT, CONSEQUEN-TIAL, SPECIAL, OR EXEMPLARY DAMAGES OR LOST PROFITS, IN EITHER CASE, IN ANY ACTION ARISING FROM OR RELATED TO THIS AGREEMENT, WHETHER BASED IN CONTRACT OR TORT (INCLUDING NEGLIGENCE).

Rules of the Road

The last bucket of contract provisions that we will review includes what I refer to as the "rules of the road." These are the various provisions that the parties agree on with respect to the existence and interpretation of the contract and include definitions, term/termination clauses, and the "boilerplate" or "miscellaneous" provisions typically located at the end of the agreement, such as governing law, notice provisions, and assignability standards. The former clauses (definitions and term/termination) are more intimately integrated into and affect the performance of the agreement. The latter are used primarily for interpretive and dispute resolution purposes.

Definitions

I always found drafting definitions to be the most fun part of putting a contract together. If a contract is a giant puzzle, then definitions are the pieces that integrate and link each different part together. If the definition is not correct, then the puzzle falls apart. Therefore, please do not be shy about pressing your client for sufficient detail to be able to draft precise definitions, and explain to them how definitions function. I also found it helpful to educate less sophisticated clients on the purpose of capitalizing defined terms (so readers know when to use the definition for the defined word) and that simply capitalizing a term (without including a corresponding definition) does not give it extra import in the contract. An undefined capitalized term simply sows confusion and, certainly, having a definition does not necessarily beget importance. When done right, it just makes for ease of reading. The more your client knows about how the contract comes together and why the questions you are asking are important, the more helpful the client's answers are likely to be.

Part of the trick in drafting definitions is separating out the actual definition from the context in which it is used. A properly crafted definition should not include any provisions relating to performance or risk shifting. Substantive clauses should go into the operative parts of the contract (covenants or risk-shifting terms) to have their intended effect.

Do	Don't
Definition of Intellectual Property: **"Intellectual Property"** means all inventions and work product developed by Consultant under this Agreement. *Representations and Warranties:* Consultant represents and warrants that all Intellectual Property is free and clear of any liens.	*Definition of Intellectual Property:* **"Intellectual Property"** means all inventions and work product developed by Consultant under this Agreement, all of which are free and clear of any liens.

It is easy to make errors when drafting definitions. But unlike the more substantive terms of the contract, the impact of a typo in a definition can have a ripple effect throughout the entire agreement, so proofreading is extra, extra important here. In the following table, take a look at some common definitions and how they are commonly mis-drafted.

Do	Don't	Mistake
"Intellectual Property Rights" has the meaning provided in Section 2.	**"Intellectual Property Rights"** has the meaning provided in Section 2, all of which are valid and subsisting on the Closing Date.	"All of which are valid and subsisting" is a substantive term that most likely belongs in the representations and warranties.
"Commercially Reasonable Efforts" means efforts that are commercially reasonable but in no event require the making of material payments or material concessions.	**"Commercially Reasonable Efforts"** and **"Best Efforts"** mean efforts that are commercially reasonable but in no event require the making of material payments or material concessions.	Only one defined term should be used for a definition.
"Company Products" means all of the products and services currently sold, licensed, or otherwise exploited by Fitness Feet.	**"Company Products"** is all of the products and services currently sold, licensed, or otherwise exploited by Fitness Feet.	Use "means" to signal a definition, not "is."
"Intellectual Property" means Technology and Intellectual Property Rights.	**"Intellectual property"** means Technology and Intellectual Property Rights.	Both "Intellectual" and "Property" should be capitalized.

Term and Termination

The other more substantive provisions in the "Rules of the Road" bucket are the Term and Termination clauses. These are, in many cases, the most straightforward to draft. You just want to make sure you have confirmed with your client the desired term of the agreement (which is often already agreed upon with the other side) and any desired termination provisions (other than for breach). This is easier said than done. Consider the following typical exchange with Fitness Feet.

You write to Casey: "Hi Casey, I wanted to confirm how long you want the Sporty Supply contract to last and whether you'd like it to auto-renew."[28]

Casey responds: "Let's do three years upfront then auto-renewals, and we want to be able to get out at any time."

Your brow furrows. Does Fitness Feet mean

1. Three-year initial term, with three-year renewal terms, but Fitness Feet can terminate for convenience at any time during the entire term?
2. Three-year initial term, with three-year renewal terms, but Fitness Feet can terminate for convenience only during the renewal terms?
3. Three-year initial term, with one-year renewal terms (it is common to lower the renewal term to one year), but Fitness Feet can terminate for convenience at any time during the entire term?
4. Three-year initial term, with one-year renewal terms, but Fitness Feet can terminate for convenience only during renewals?

You have a couple of options. You can make a guess at which of the four options Casey intended, or you can go back to the client for clarity. Which approach do you think is more efficient?

If you guessed the latter, then you are correct. It is *far* more efficient to get the right facts from your client up front then guess, be wrong, and have to go back to the drawing board. Additionally, getting back to the client with the four different plausible interpretations gives the client an opportunity to think about some nuances it might not have previously considered, such as that the renewal term may differ from

---

[28] "Auto-renewals" refers to the practice of an agreement automatically renewing at a certain frequency unless a party takes an action to terminate the agreement. The contract is typically drafted to say: "The term of this Agreement is X years (the '**Initial Term**'). After the Initial Term, this Agreement will automatically renew for successive [Y-month] terms (each, a '**Renewal Term**' and with the Initial Term, the '**Term**') until either party provides notice of nonrenewal to the other party at least [Z] days prior to the end of the then current Initial Term or Renewal Term, as applicable."

the initial term, or that a right to terminate for convenience can kick in at some period after the beginning of the contract.

You write back to Fitness Feet:

"Thanks! A three-year initial term sounds good for a relationship like this one.[29] I have just a couple of questions for clarification:

- Do you want each renewal term to be three years long? This would mean that if you do not terminate at the end of the initial term, you are signing up for another three years (although it sounds like you want to be able to get out at any time). You can always go back with one- or two-year renewal terms if three years makes you uncomfortable.

- Do you want the right to terminate for convenience to kick in immediately or just during renewal terms? If the former, then the issue of a set term becomes a bit of a fiction since you can get out at any time. If the latter, then Sporty Supply might be okay with it if we build in an appropriate notice period. Alternatively, if you are going back with one-year renewal terms, could you get comfortable with a right to get out of the contract only upon conclusion of the annual renewal terms (versus anytime)? I suspect that will be the most palatable approach to Sporty Supply, but happy to go with whatever you prefer."

Fitness Feet's response is characteristic of a client on the receiving end of so much helpful feedback: "Thanks so much for that information! You're right, it doesn't make a lot of sense to have auto-renewals with a broad right to also terminate for convenience anytime. I like your suggestion of one-year auto-renewals after the three-year term. Let's make the renewal notice period ninety days and do away with the right to terminate any time."

This sort of exchange, which I had dozens of times while representing start-ups, does more than just clarify what terms to draft into the contract. It sets up a collaborative dynamic between you and the client, pursuant to which you can help guide your client's thinking and understanding of what is typical. Developing a solid relationship stems from listening to what the client wants, giving some meaningful thought to it, validating the client's ask, and then seeking clarification and making recommendations for tweaks. This sort of collaboration on finding the right terms and approach for a given deal is what computers and

---

[29] Manufacturing relationships often require significant investment from each party to get up and running, so it could be a few months into the contract before product is being produced.

artificial intelligence cannot replicate and what the subsequent chapters focus on.

Boilerplate

A confession—I hate referring to the "miscellaneous" or "general" provisions at the back of most contracts as "boilerplate." The term suggests that those sections are truly standard, drafted in only one way, are never changed, and are not prone to errors, all of which is wrong. Nevertheless, given how common the term is (particularly among clients), I will use it here.

When I say "boilerplate," I mean the last one or two pages of a contract (or longer, in some more sophisticated deals) that customarily include the following provisions: Assignment, Entire Agreement (which may also be referred to as the "integration" or "merger" clause), Amendments, Waivers, Counterparts, Severability, Headings, Governing Law/Venue, and Notices.

Many of these provisions are, indeed, fairly standard. I am hard pressed to find an example of a time when I negotiated the Counterparts paragraph (which clarifies the agreement may be signed in two separate "counterparts," e.g., separate PDFs rather than wet ink signatures on the same page). The same is true for the clause that requires amendments to the agreement be made in writing. It provides certainty to both parties that neither can vary the terms of the agreement orally—both parties are usually comfortable with that construct. We will zero in, however, on three of the boilerplate provisions that often are negotiated or at least may vary significantly between deals. Knowing when and how to conform these provisions to the matter at hand and how to explain to your client why they need some thought will help chip away at the mistaken belief that these provisions are standard.

Assignment

→ *Neither party may assign this Agreement without the other party's prior, written consent.*

We start with the boilerplate provision that is probably the most negotiated, impactful, and integral to deals—Assignment (or Anti-Assignment). When I started practicing, I had no idea the assignment clause had any importance, and yet, it is one of the most consequential provisions for business lawyers. Clients similarly often lack an understanding of why getting this provision right matters, which is where you come in.

Further, assignment provisions in contracts do not just come up in the course of a negotiation. Once agreed to, they will pop up all of the time over the course of a company's life. Assignment clauses in important contracts will be analyzed for due diligence in financings and acquisitions and be considered at board of directors' meetings when determining whether a potential acquirer is likely to see those contracts as roadblocks. Getting ahead of those future headaches at the point of drafting and negotiation is a significant and well-received investment in your relationship with your client.

Assignment clauses set forth the situations in which a party may (or may not) assign or transfer its rights and/or obligations under the agreement to a third party. These clauses come in many shapes and sizes—a table later in this section sets forth many examples. Some may simply prohibit assignment of the agreement without consent, like the previous example, while others can be rather complex, setting forth specific situations, such as an internal business reorganization, in which assignment is permissible.

Assignments to unrelated third parties are not particularly common. Rather, the language used in the assignment clause frequently becomes important in the context where an assignment is most likely to occur: a merger or acquisition of a party to the contract. As described later, some M&A transactions result in assignments of those contracts, and simply put, how an assignment provision is drafted in a client's business agreements can impact whether your client can go forward with a successful exit opportunity—or not.

If the assignment provision is a simple prohibition on assignment, as set forth at the beginning of this section, then your client is likely in the clear for exit opportunities if the structure of the acquisition does not result in an assignment of contracts to which the client is a party. Let's break that down. There are many different ways an acquisition can be structured. Parties choose different structures for various reasons, the primary one often being tax related. Reverse triangular mergers, forward triangular mergers, stock purchases, and asset acquisitions are the most common forms of M&A, with the reverse triangular merger proving to be the most used.[30] In a reverse triangular merger, the acquired company remains in existence at the end of the transaction. It merges into a shell company, and the shell company disappears, leaving the acquired company in place with the same name and corporate organization, just a different owner.

Most courts presented with the question of whether a reverse triangular merger results in an assignment of contracts to which the

---

[30] Kevin Tsai, *Selling Your Company: Merger vs. Stock Sale vs. Asset Sale*, COOLEY GO, https://www.cooleygo.com/selling-your-company-merger-vs-stock-sale-vs-asset-sale/.

acquired party is a party have held that it does not.[31] The surviving entity is the same company that existed prior to the acquisition, so there is no "assignment" between companies. A similar rationale applies to a purchase of all of a company's stock or equity. There is a change of ownership (referred to as a "change of control") at a level above the acquired company, but the acquired company remains the same; as a result, courts have held that no assignment of contracts to which that acquired company is a party has occurred.

However, contrast the reverse triangular merger and stock purchase with the two other possible acquisition formats: an acquisition of a company's assets or a forward triangular merger. In these transaction structures, assignments *do* result from the deal. In an asset acquisition, certain assets, which may include contracts, are transferred between two companies. The companies themselves do not merge. Forward triangular mergers are the opposite of reverse triangular mergers: the acquired company merges into the shell company, and the acquired company disappears, leaving the shell company. In both cases, the target company is no longer the holder of the contracts to which it was originally a party.

To sum up, all four of the transaction structures described result in a "change of control," but only two are likely to result in de facto assignments of contracts to which the acquired company is a party.

Now, let's consider how the contract language around assignability in a bilateral business deal becomes an issue in these scenarios. If a provision simply prohibits assignment without consent (like the example at the beginning of this section), then an acquired company will probably not need to seek consent from the counterparty in a reverse triangular merger or a stock purchase. There is no per se assignment in those situations. Consent would certainly be required, however, for the other two deal formats.

Consent, to be clear, is a real issue. If a party is required to seek consent from various business partners (whether those business partners are easy-going and reasonable, or not), the closing of the acquisition will be delayed if the target company cannot obtain the consents in a timely manner. Further, it may open itself up to renegotiations with the parties from whom consent is sought, especially on economic terms

---

[31] There are a couple of outlier court cases that have held a reverse triangular merger can result in an assignment of a contract where that contract is a license agreement and the acquired company is the licensee. *See, e.g.,* SQL Solutions, Inc. v. Oracle Corp., 1991 WL 626458 (N.D. Cal. Dec. 19, 1991). However, this approach has been rebutted by other courts. *See, e.g.,* Meso Scale Diagnostics, LLC v. Roche Diagnostics GMBH, 62 A.3d 62 (Del. Ch. 2013).

(some parties may want money in exchange for the consent). Moreover, an acquired company's failure to obtain consent from key business partners can kill an acquisition completely. The best assignment provisions are those that allow the client to proceed with an exit without having to seek consent.

For clients who are likely to seek exits through M&A activity, it is so necessary to maintain their right to freely assign the agreement in the event of a change of control that in circumstances where that client has very little leverage (imagine representing Fitness Feet in a deal with Apple), you might spend 100% of your negotiation capital ensuring consent will not be required (imagine trying to seek consent from Apple). But if you are negotiating *against* a venture-backed company and are worried about one of your competitors buying that company (i.e., you are Apple negotiating against Fitness Feet and are worried Google might buy Fitness Feet), you may want to try and prevent that situation from happening by prohibiting a change of control to an acquirer without your consent.

When crafting assignment provisions, careful drafters must consider the chance that their clients, and the counterparties to their clients' contracts, might be acquired and adjust the language accordingly. If the lawyer knows there is a high likelihood that the counterparty to their client's deal will be acquired by their client's competitor (and your client does not want to be in business with a competitor), then the lawyer needs to address that scenario in the draft. If the client is likely to seek a buyer in the near term, then the attorney needs to account for that, too. There are many ways to draft around these various scenarios. The most common are set forth in the following chart.

	Sample Assignment Language	Reverse Triangular Merger	Forward Triangular Merger	Stock Purchase	Asset Purchase
1	Company may freely assign this Agreement.	No consent needed.	No consent needed.	No consent needed.	No consent needed.
2	Company may not assign this Agreement without Other Party's prior, written consent.	Consent likely not needed.	Consent required.	No consent needed.	Consent required.

(Continued)

	Sample Assignment Language	Reverse Triangular Merger	Forward Triangular Merger	Stock Purchase	Asset Purchase
3	Company may not assign this Agreement without Other Party's prior, written consent, including by way of a change of control.[32]	Consent may be required.	Consent required.	Consent may be required.	Consent required.
4	Company may not assign this Agreement without Other Party's prior, written consent, except that no such consent is required in the event of a change of control.	No consent needed.	No consent needed.	No consent needed.	No consent needed.
5	Company may assign this Agreement without Other Party's prior, written consent, except in the event of a change of control (including a stock purchase or merger) to an entity that is a competitor of Other Party.	No consent needed, unless acquirer is a competitor of Other Party.	No consent needed, unless acquirer is a competitor of Other Party.	No consent needed, unless acquirer is a competitor of Other Party.	No consent needed, unless acquirer is a competitor of Other Party.

[32] This particular provision often becomes the source of heavy negotiation in an M&A deal, which can be easily avoided with some clearer drafting. By adding "including by way of a change of control," the drafter opens up a path to two different interpretations: (1) all changes of control (including those that do not constitute assignments, such as reverse triangular mergers and stock purchases) will require consent or (2) only changes of control that actually result in an assignment require consent. Typically, a drafter intends for the former with this provision (an astute drafter will not call out "change of control" unless they truly want to wrap in all of the various forms of a change of control) and should resolve the future ambiguity by stating in the draft: ". . . including by way of a change of control (including a reverse triangular merger and stock purchase agreement)."

This chart is just the tip of the iceberg of the different levers you can pull in drafting and negotiating assignment language based on your client's situation, potential acquirers, leverage, and competitive landscape. In addition to the anti-assignment mechanics, you may also see (and consider) termination rights associated with different kinds of changes of control, allowing a party to terminate the agreement if the other party is acquired. In terms of analysis for exit scenarios, a termination provision may be just as thorny as an anti-assignment clause.

There are few greater value-adds to a client than the ability to articulate how the terms they agree to in the short term will affect their long-term growth, and assignability is a key area to focus in on when doing that analysis. Your client's main focus is on economics and the terms governing how to operationalize each business relationship. When you flag these nonobvious issues that can have outsized consequences for your client and explain why they are important, you are demonstrating an interest in your client's future prospects and ability to conduct and grow its business in the future, and not just the deal at hand.

The negotiation of an assignment clause is a crystal clear example of how counseling for a long-term relationship is a successful attorney's key function that cannot be automated away. For instance, it is easy to distinguish between the first two clauses in the previous chart—prohibiting all assignments that occur by all means, and freely allowing all assignments by any means. As you move down the chart, the fact pattern that is specific to your client's circumstances at a given time will dictate where you land and how you advise your client.

Exercise 2-8:

Casey has informed you that Sporty Supply is very concerned that Fitness Feet is on a "unicorn" path and may be acquired by any of the other, larger wearable tracker manufacturers that Sporty Supply competes with. Fitness Feet is also confident in its trajectory but has little interest in being acquired by a manufacturer. It's holding out for one of the more legendary "big tech" companies to come along with a billion-dollar check. Which of the assignment provisions in the previous chart would be a good compromise position for you to recommend offering to Sporty Supply that will give them the comfort they are looking for in addition to the opportunities Fitness Feet is primarily focused on?

_____

_____

_____

The two other boilerplate clauses that are most likely to trigger some negotiation are the governing law/venue and the notice provisions. Fortunately, both of those are usually much easier to come to agreement on than the assignment section.

Governing Law/Venue

As you learned in your first-year law school (1L) courses, the law governing the interpretation of a contract must relate, in some way, to the parties or the performance of the contract. Similarly, the chosen venue to resolve disputes should also be related. If neither of the "home" states of the parties (i.e., where each party's main business operations is located) is agreeable, then Delaware is a common compromise because it has a large body of corporate law and most companies are incorporated as Delaware corporations. For the same reasons, New York (if it is neither party's home state) is often used. As a general rule, the chosen venue should be the courts of the state whose law will govern—the best interpreters of a given body of law are those that do it every day.

If the parties cannot agree on a chosen law and/or venue, you can recommend arbitration, but make sure your client understands the risks and benefits. Arbitration is less expensive, usually more expedient, and confidential—all of which may incentivize a party to formalize disputes. Litigation is the exact opposite in all three respects but, as a result, may also deter formalizing disputes and encourage parties to work things out on their own.[33]

Notices

The Notices provision is perhaps the most mechanical (and, to be honest, most mundane) of all contract provisions, spelling out how and when notices between the parties are to be given. Boring, right? Yet very important. "Notices" are, among other things, how parties find out their indemnification obligations may be triggered and how they effectuate termination in a manner permitted under the agreement.

To ensure that a client will receive and be able to give the notices required under the contract in a timely manner, a lawyer should ask which circumstances in the contract require notices and what form of notice would be sufficient for those circumstances. For example, if the only required notice in the contract relates to indemnification obligations, then a lawyer and client might be comfortable with a more formal mailing mechanism, such as certified or registered mail. If there are

---

[33] Note that this rationale is consistent throughout the United States but not necessarily in other jurisdictions.

many different provisions requiring notices, then the client may want the flexibility to exchange some or all notices via email, which is becoming increasingly common.

With respect to email notices, lawyers must think through what it truly means to send legal notifications via email. Emails are fraught with the potential of being caught in a spam filter, accidentally deleted, ignored, or a recipient may be out of the office and have automatic replies enabled. As clients opt for email notices more often, it would be prudent to consider how to ensure those notices do not take effect until actually read and received. For example, you could state that the notice is not effective until the recipient confirms reply by phone or nonautomatic email. You could also require notices sent by email also be sent by a more formal means, such as certified mail, and that the effective date of the notice is the date of receipt of the physical mail. In effect, the email notice is a courtesy. Ultimately, it is the client's choice, and you should ask which the client prefers depending on the circumstances for which notices are required.

Boilerplate Wrap-Up

When it comes to drafting the boilerplate, as with the rest of the contract, the goal is to be clear and concise. Other than the assignability clause, which can have a material effect on a company's ability to facilitate an exit, boilerplate provisions are mostly administrative or interpretive, setting forth the rules of the contract's performance and interpretation. Other attorneys (whether your successor at your firm, opposing counsel, or litigators trying to understand the contract in the case of a dispute several years later) and clients do not want to spend their time figuring out basic interpretive rules, such as where a lawsuit should be filed or how to send a notice of an indemnifiable claim. Rather, their time should be spent analyzing the operative parts of the contract to determine whether a claim is viable, or a breach has actually occurred. As such, ambiguity is rarely your friend when drafting boilerplate. Draft as if a nonlawyer client will need to be able to read and understand these provisions without any assistance from an attorney.

When it comes to the tone you take, pragmatism will carry the day so long as you are careful in ensuring the specifics of the deal are reflected and you are not hindering your client's business. It can be very easy to "copy and paste" from a precedent and forget to reread the various provisions to make sure they make sense in the context of each deal. Yet, a savvy client will know if you grafted in a precedent provision without making changes. Even if the rest of the contract is perfectly drafted, if you have forgotten to change the governing law from New York to Georgia for your Atlanta-based client, your client will notice—and wonder why they are paying hundreds of dollars an hour to read your work and find careless mistakes. Make sure you do a careful proofread of these provisions before finalizing your draft. Just one cautious read can pick up some notable changes.

Exercise 2-9:

Following are some notes you took during a phone call with Casey from Fitness Feet about the Sporty Supply deal and some sections from a precedent agreement Ashley has provided you to use. Use the notes to identify where you need to make changes to the precedent language.

Your Call Notes:

- FF is talking to a few potential acquirers—need M&A flexibility.

- CA law (Sporty based in San Diego). Prefer venue in San Francisco.

- Add email notices. No need for fax.

Precedent Language:
Assignment. Neither party may assign this Agreement without the other party's prior, written consent.

Describe Changes:

_____

_____

Governing Law. This agreement is governed by New York law. The parties consent to the state and federal courts located in New York County as the exclusive venue for any actions, suits, or other proceedings arising out of or relating to this Agreement.

Describe Changes:

_____

_____

Notices. Any notice, payment, demand, or other communication required or permitted to be delivered or given by the provisions of this Agreement will be deemed to have been effectively delivered and received (i) if personally delivered, upon receipt; (ii) if sent via facsimile, upon telephone confirmation of receipt; or (iii) if sent by registered or certified mail, five days after deposit in the US mail and, in each case, addressed to the parties at the addresses set forth in the signature block.

Describe Changes:

_____

_____

Organizing Information

Now that you know how the skeleton of a contract comes together, when you are beginning work on a project, think about what sort of contract provision is the best fit for each fact based on how contract performance is intended to occur, the potential remedy (or remedies) for breach, and industry custom. Some details may end up in multiple buckets. We have already looked at how facts can be reflected in both representations and warranties, as well as covenants. There are numerous other combinations of contract provisions where certain items may end up depending on what kind of promise or assurance your client wants and what remedy the client might want to seek. As we continue our journey with the Fitness Feet projects, we will review different ways to organize your information as you think these things through.

Before we move onto the drafting process and how to engage your client in that process, let's try one last exercise to illuminate how you might organize the information provided to you.

Exercise 2-10:

Following is an email you receive from Casey at Fitness Feet regarding their Easy Exercise deal. Identify the bucket of contract provision (covenants, risk-shifting provisions, rules of the road) for each numbered fact in the following bullet list.

"Hey there, I know we've spent a bunch of time on Sporty Supply, but we need to pick up that Easy Exercise deal again. Just to recap where we left off:

- We are providing Easy Exercise with fifty gift cards for our trackers (1).

- Easy Exercise is going to give away the gift cards to its members (2).

- Easy Exercise is going to do some email and social media promo around the giveaway (3).

We've talked a bit more with Easy Exercise and would like to also cover these terms in the contract:

- Easy Exercise is going to do a sweepstakes-style giveaway for the gift cards. We know there are a bunch of laws around that sort of stuff, so we need to make sure that they are in compliance with those (4), and if we get sued because they messed it up, they'll pay for our costs (5). There can be hefty fines in those lawsuits, so let's make sure we'll be able to get a full recovery (6).

- This is a short-term partnership, we just want it to last for three months (7).

- We agreed that it is in our interest to also promote the partnership, so we'll agree to do so some social media posts, as well (8).

- Our investors want us to start thinking about an exit, so we need to make sure there's nothing in here that would be an obstacle to an acquisition (9)."

Chapter 2 Wrap-Up

Strategies for Success

Contract Provisions Drafting Checklist

Following is a checklist of questions to consider to help your drafting for each contract component. The client's responses to these questions will guide your thinking as you begin to draft an agreement.

Covenants

1. What is each party obligated to do under the contract (and how, when, and where)?
2. What is each party providing the other party under the contract (and how, when, and where)?

Risk-Shifting

3. What assurances does your client need about the party's operation of its business in the past, present, and future?
4. What plausible claims might be brought by a third party for which you will want to be insured against?
5. What claims is your client comfortable providing an indemnification for?
6. Is there an easily ascertainable value of the contract that you can tie a liability cap to? If not, should you consider insurance limits/ deductibles?
7. What sort of claims should logically be excluded from the limitation on liability?

Rules of the Road

8. Do all capitalized terms in the agreement have a definition?
9. Have you used each defined term at least once so that you don't have extraneous definitions?
10. Is there one defined term for each definition?
11. Have you been consistent in your drafting of the definitions (i.e., using "'[Defined Term]' means" . . . for each defined term)?
12. Do you know the term of the contract? Are there any special termination rights you should account for?
13. Does your client need a right to freely assign the agreement, or assign in the event of an M&A event (for venture-backed companies, this is a necessity).

14. Is the governing law logical given the parties and circumstances of the deal?
15. Did you check to see if your client wants to be able to send and receive legal notices via email?
16. Do you have severability, waiver, amendment, counterparts, and integration clauses?

Chapter 2

Sample Exercise Responses

Exercise 2-1:

Example A:

1. Billy Joel will perform at Madison Square Garden on November 12, 2021, at 7:30 p.m.
2. Madison Square Garden Productions will pay Billy Joel $250,000 no later than three days before the performance and $250,000 within three days after the performance.
3. Billy Joel will perform at least four top-ten singles.

Example B:

1. Consultant will perform the software engineering services set forth on the Statement of Work.
2. Fitness Feet will pay Consultant $20 per hour.
3. Fitness Feet will make available relevant senior members of its engineering team.

Exercise 2-2:

1. Sporty Supply will supply fitness trackers (consideration).
2. Fitness Feet will pay $10 per tracker (consideration).
3. Fitness Feet will issue purchase orders each month.
4. Sporty Supply will issue an invoice after Fitness Feet accepts the trackers.
5. Fitness Feet will pay Sporty Supply within thirty days of the date of invoice.
6. Sporty Supply may not supply trackers to Fitness Feet's competitors during the Agreement.

Exercise 2-3:

1. Sporty Supply will manufacture and supply the trackers in accordance with the purchase orders issued by Fitness Feet.
2. Fitness Feet will issue purchase orders to Sporty Supply on a monthly basis.
3. Fitness Feet will pay Sporty Supply $10 per tracker within thirty days of the date of invoice. Alternatively, you could split this covenant into two separate covenants: Fitness Feet will pay Sporty Supply $10 per tracker.
   Fitness Feet will pay Sporty Supply within thirty days of receipt of an invoice.
4. Sporty Supply will issue an invoice for each shipment after Fitness Feet accepts that shipment of trackers.
5. Sporty Supply will not supply Fitness Feet's competitors during the term of the Agreement.

Exercise 2-4:

Fitness Feet grants Sporty Supply a license to Fitness Feet's logo for the sole purpose of manufacturing and branding Fitness Feet's trackers with Fitness Feet's logo pursuant to the terms of this Agreement.

Exercise 2-5:

1. Noninfringement of intellectual property rights, because Fitness Feet cannot enter into this deal without assurances that Sporty Supply's conduct will not infringe a third party's rights (such as patents) in the manufacture of the trackers.
2. The trackers are made in compliance with applicable laws.
3. Sporty Supply has no agreements that would conflict with its obligations under the Fitness Feet agreement, because Fitness Feet will want to know if Sporty Supply cannot agree to the exclusivity being requested.
4. The trackers are and will be free from material defects.

Exercise 2-6:

Hopefully your list included any or all of the following: intellectual property infringement, product liability claims, and negligence or willful misconduct in carrying out its obligations.

Exercise 2-7:

A cap tied to the amounts Fitness Feet has paid or owes Sporty Supply would be typical here, such as the "fees Fitness Feet has paid or owes Sporty Supply for trackers provided in the 12 months prior to the date giving rise to the claim."

Exercise 2-8:

I would offer the provision in row 5, which allows Fitness Feet to transfer the agreement in the event of a change of control but excludes changes of control to competitors of Sporty Supply. Drafting this sort of provision shows Fitness Feet (and Sporty Supply) that you are trying to help them get the deal across the finish line while preserving Fitness Feet's most likely exit options.

Exercise 2-9:

The edited precedent would reflect the following changes:

Assignment. Neither party may assign this Agreement without the other party's prior, written consent; provided, however, that Fitness Feet may assign this Agreement without Sporty Supply's consent in the event of a merger, acquisition, or purchase of all or substantially all of Fitness Feet's assets.

Governing Law. This Agreement is governed by ~~New York~~ California law. The parties consent to the state and federal courts located in ~~New York~~ San Francisco County as the exclusive venue for any actions, suits, or other proceedings arising out of or relating to this Agreement.

Notices. Any notice, payment, demand, or other communication required or permitted to be delivered or given by the provisions of this Agreement will be deemed to have been effectively delivered and received (i) if personally delivered, upon receipt; (ii) if sent via email, upon nonautomatic email reply confirming receipt ~~facsimile, upon telephone confirmation of receipt~~; or (iii) if sent by registered or certified mail, five days after deposit in the US mail and, in each case, addressed to the parties at the addresses set forth in the signature block.

Exercise 2-10:

1. Covenant
2. Covenant
3. Covenant
4. Risk Shifting (Representation and Warranty)
5. Risk Shifting (Indemnification)
6. Risk Shifting (Limitation on Liability)
7. Rules of the Road (Term)
8. Covenant
9. Rules of the Road (Assignment)

Chapter 3

Clearing Conflicts: A Useful Proxy for Difficult Conversations

> **Step 1:**
> **Clearing**
> **Conflicts**

W e dive into our drafting projects by picking up where you left off in your conversation with Ashley about Fitness Feet in Chapter 1. If you recall, Ashley had asked if you had any questions about your initial assignments.

Gulp. "Uh, no, I don't think so," you reply. You quickly cycle through the different housekeeping items you learned in firm orientation, and just as Ashley is leaving your office, you remember hearing something about ethics. "Wait! Just one question for now—do we need to run a conflicts check?"

"Yes!" Ashley walks back into your office. "Thanks for remembering; it's easy to forget. You'll need to confirm the legal name for Easy Exercise—I mean, if it's an LLC or Inc. or if 'Easy Exercise' is just a DBA[1]—with the client and then you can run the check or ask your assistant to help."

---

[1] A "doing business as" (DBA) name is a name that a company uses publicly but is not the same as the company's legal name.

With that exchange, we zero in on the first meaningful step for any new project. Anytime a lawyer is engaged to draft a bilateral agreement with an identifiable adverse party (as opposed to drafting, for example, online terms of service, consumer warranties, or board minutes), then they must ensure there are no ethical obstacles to helping with the deal. You clear this hurdle by running a "conflicts check" on the counterparty in accordance with your firm's protocol.

We are starting with conflicts checks because attorneys *cannot* proceed with matters unless they are ethically cleared to do so. This applies to all lawyers, at all levels (from first-year associate to seasoned partner, whether at a solo law practice or a giant law firm). And this is not just "best practice"—state bar ethics rules typically require *all* attorneys to run conflicts checks on *all* adverse parties.

Before discussing how to handle conflicts-related issues with a client (including messaging), let's quickly review some basic principles (noting, of course, that your state bar ethics rules may vary slightly):

1. If you are going to be adverse to another current client of your current firm (even if you do not work on that current client's matters or were not even aware they were a client), then you need a waiver from that current client. You also need to disclose the conflict to your client in writing (via email is usually fine, although some firms require certain forms or letters). Your firm should set up an "ethical wall" to avoid disclosures (intentional or not) between the different client teams.[2]

2. If you are going to be representing a client adverse to a prior client of your current firm, then you need to disclose to your client that the counterparty was a prior client, and you should avoid having attorneys who worked on the prior client be involved in your project.[3]

Again, always check your firm's own policies and procedures (and state law) for any variances from these points, and do not be shy about calling your firm's general counsel's office for advice, if you have one. Big law firms have their own general counsels to help you (and the firm) avoid incurring legal liability relating to practicing law. Questions about how to manage or identify conflicts fit squarely within that mission, and it is great to build a relationship with that team so that when you have a real emergency, they will be able to effectively help you.

---

2 *See, e.g.,* N.Y. Rules of Prof'l Conduct R1.7, 1.8, 1.10.
3 *See, e.g., id.,* R1.9, 1.10.

In my experience, however, not all attorneys or practices are vigilant in clearing conflicts. This can lead to real issues, and even the most diligent of lawyers can make a mistake. It's best to err on the side of caution when it comes to ethics.

Real-World Example: When I was a senior associate, I lateraled from one firm to another. In that process, I brought clients with me that I had worked with for several years.

One of those clients, Company A, was my most active client—they required significant hours of my time every week, and I had spent years developing my relationship with them. In return, they saw me as a trusted advisor who had deep institutional knowledge of their business and considered me part of the "team."

At my prior firm, Company A and I had begun working on a project adverse to a large corporation, Company B. I planned on continuing that project when I joined the second firm and was eager to pick up where I left off when I joined. Conflicts at the prior firm had been cleared through the normal channels.

During the time when I transitioned between firms, the project had moved along from a business standpoint, and the parties were ready to start papering the deal. Company A reached out to me on my first day of work at my new firm to schedule a negotiation and finalize the terms. We got the call on the calendar for the following week.

One hour before the negotiation was scheduled to begin, it occurred to me that I had failed to run a conflicts check at my new firm. I submitted an urgent request, praying for an "all clear." Unfortunately, however, Company B was a client of my new firm in unrelated matters. I went into panic mode—I was ethically prohibited from getting on the negotiation, and I only had an hour to let the parties know and figure out what to do.

Ultimately, I had to cancel on the client, owning up to my own mistake and letting them know that we would work to clear the conflict as quickly as possible. Like many clients, their response was to ask if this was "a real issue"—they had never run into a conflicts issue before and didn't see why it was a problem since I personally was not going to do any work for Company B.

It was a real issue, unfortunately, I explained. I could not violate the state bar rules, and I hoped that the lawyers on the other side would understand my predicament. Further, with the client's interests in mind, I had to advise Company A that their best immediate option was to call the lawyers at my prior firm to see if they could hop on the negotiation in the next hour. They had enough background from working with me on the project before I quit, and we knew conflicts was not an issue there.

I lost that project completely, along with some of the trust I had worked so hard to build with Company A. Running conflicts has to be at the top of your mind because if you blow it (as I did), your client relationships can truly suffer.

To avoid issues like the one I found myself in, and other future headaches, it is best to get in the habit from the outset of making sure that you are cleared to continue for every project. After all, you have worked really hard to be able to practice law. Anytime a lawyer skimps on the conflicts check or assumes that someone else ran the check, they put all that hard work at risk. If you are a solo practitioner, I would caution against relying on your memory to determine if you have done work for a particular company and encourage you to formalize a process. Investing in a simple software solution while you are small will also allow you to scale your business (if you choose to) more easily in the future.

Running a Conflicts Check

So what does running a conflicts check look like? It varies from firm to firm, but generally, attorneys submit requests via email or through an online portal with the client's name, the adverse party's legal name, and the nature of the project (e.g., "drafting a short partnership agreement" or "investor in venture round"). In return, a report is generated that indicates whether the other party is a current or former client of the firm, or neither.

Conflicts reports can be confusing at first. It will pay dividends to spend five minutes with a partner or a conflicts attorney learning how to interpret it when you first join. Many associates often have their assistants help with conflicts check. If you take that route, remember that as the lawyer it is your ultimate responsibility to make sure the conflict is cleared. You should know how to read the report.

Communicating with Your Client

As the starting point for any new assignment or client, clearing conflicts also presents the first opportunity for an attorney to show a client how they will approach the relationship going forward. Lawyers must communicate with clients about the conflicts checks process, and how that is accomplished can set them up for success (or failure) throughout the entire relationship because news about running a conflicts check is not always welcome.

A conflicts check introduces an unknown step in the process that may affect timing expectations. When clients reach out for help with an agreement, they usually want to get started right away, and many will not expect that there could be delay due to legal ethics rules they have never heard of. As a result, how you communicate this somewhat unwelcome news can really impact the dynamic between you and the client. To get ahead of the future headache that will come from not managing the client's expectations, we will review some principles about drafting emails. These guidelines apply to all email communications, and I encourage you to bookmark them for future use.

Drafting Effective Emails

In drafting any email to a client, your tone is as important as the message.[4] This is especially true when the message concerns a topic that is likely to be unfamiliar to a client. As such, when talking about something as "lawyerly" as conflicts checks, be mindful that there is a lot that clients do not know about practicing law, and they certainly do not have visibility into your own firm guidelines and requirements around new projects and clients. Nonlawyers may not know what is meant by a "conflicts check." Even when representing clients that have in-house lawyers, never assume that *your* ethical obligations are at top of mind or that the in-house lawyer has prior firm experience. Therefore, it is incumbent on you to take care to explain what a conflicts check is and why you need to run it.

The substance of the message must make clear that anytime you are adverse to another company, you have to make sure that company is not also a client of your firm *because* there are rules preventing lawyers from being adverse to other firm clients without a waiver. The "because" clause is important; it signals that this process is out of your control and therefore nonnegotiable.

It may feel uncomfortable at first to tell a client that you cannot start on a matter until the conflicts process is complete (especially in a service industry where accommodating client requests is a big part of the job). Delivering unwanted news is almost always uncomfortable. However, if you phrase the email correctly, this first exchange with the client

---

4 This also applies to emails sent to adverse parties, lawyers, or colleagues—everyone you communicate with professionally (and personally).

can be used to demonstrate that, while the conflicts check must be run, you are already thinking past it to the bigger picture and project.

First, transparency builds trust. A foundation for trust is laid by bringing the client in on your process through describing that conflicts must be cleared and providing timing expectations so that the client has a sense of when you might be able to get started. Second, by explaining the conflicts process at the outset, you have laid the groundwork to avoid a future headache—a key component of a successful practice. In this case, the future headache is the unavoidable situation where your client has an "urgent" matter and requests an unrealistic turnaround time. When you have to respond to *that* email reminding the client that you need to go through conflicts first and that may impact the desired timeline, the client will hopefully be more understanding and less surprised if you have always been transparent about the conflicts process. In time, they may even know to build that step and the chance of a conflict into its expectations, even in a "fire drill." Last, from a practical standpoint, emailing the client about the conflicts checks gives you the opportunity to get the counterparty's legal name (necessary for the conflicts check), which you will also need to draft the contract.

Consider this sample email from you to Fitness Feet letting them know about the conflicts check process.

→ *"Thanks for reaching out. We'd love to help with the Easy Exercise partnership agreement. First, because of legal ethics rules, we need to make sure that Easy Exercise is not also a Landy Law client. Can you please let us know the gym's full legal name (e.g., "Easy Exercise Inc.")?*
  Once we have that info, we'll run a quick "conflicts check" and get back to you ASAP, typically within one day.[5] Assuming there is no conflict, then we will take an initial look and let you know what questions we have about the deal and if we think a call would be helpful. If there is a conflict, then we'll let you know what the best next steps are to clear it. In the meantime, please let me know if you have any questions about the conflicts process."

This email plainly accomplishes the objectives laid out earlier. It describes the process you are going to undertake to make sure there are no conflicts, as well as what you will do if there are conflicts. It does

---

[5] If you are going to borrow this language (which is encouraged), be sure to adjust the time frame here to mirror your own firm's usual turnaround time.

this in a clear way that the client will understand and be able to absorb easily. It also provides Fitness Feet with an estimated timeline. Telling a client there is a delay without providing an estimate for how long it will take to resolve it is a form of self-sabotage. Clients who are paying several hundred dollars an hour for your time rightly expect a certain level of responsiveness and turnaround time. It is your job to manage those expectations so they are in line with reality. This message also clearly gets you the information you need—the legal name. Compare the previous email with this alternative approach:

→ *"Thanks for reaching out. We'd love to help with the gym partnership agreement. Can you please let us know what Easy Exercise's legal name is? We'll need to run a conflicts check before we get started."*

Fitness Feet responds: *"Sure, it's Easy Exercise LLC. Can you please remind me, what is a conflicts check?"*

"Of course," you write. *"Legal ethics rules require us to make sure that the gym is not also a firm client, so we have to do a formal search of our records, which we call a 'conflicts check.'"*

"Ah, okay. How long will that take?" You hate when clients ask about timing of things that are out of your control.

"Hopefully just a day or so. Then we can get started, assuming there is no conflict," you respond.

"What happens if there is a conflict?"

. . .

You get the idea. By not anticipating (and not answering) the client's questions up front and giving them the information they need to temper their expectations, you have added several emails to your already bursting inbox, and you lost the ability to control how the information is packaged together. In the first email example, when you present all of the information up front, you can control the interweaving between "good news" ("typically within one day" and "assuming there is no conflict . . .") and bad news ("we have to run a quick conflicts check," which a client interprets as a delay, and "if there is a conflict . . ."). When you weave those different messages together, on balance, the client digests the entirety of the substance: There is a slight delay, but we're thinking long term about the project and will get you updates as soon as possible. Anytime an email message from a lawyer results in a long back-and-forth with the client about details, the lawyer has lost the ability to control how the entirety of the chain is received and interpreted, and a no-longer-avoidable now-present headache has been created. The good news and bad news are isolated from each other—and you can guess which one the client will pay more attention to.

As a lawyer, you will be giving your clients "bad news" all the time: their product proposal gives rise to significant legal liability, the way they want to price their stock options is against the law, they've been sued, and so on. That's just part of the job. And that's why excellent client service depends at least as much on how news is delivered as what the news actually is.

The other issue with the long back-and-forth is that it, frankly, wastes your and your client's time. Every time you have to read and write another email, you are losing time you can be spending on more valuable projects—like getting the conflicts check going. If you have the information on hand that you think a client will want to know, then go ahead and put it out there.

If your conflicts report comes back with a "hit" (i.e., the other party is a client of the firm), use the same method as discussed earlier in terms of transparency and balancing the bad news ("there's a conflict") with the good ("we're working on it"). That might look like the following if you were to have a conflict for Fitness Feet:

→ *"Hey Fitness Feet, thanks for providing the information about Easy Exercise. We ran conflicts, and it looks like Easy Exercise is a client of the firm. We've reached out to Easy Exercise's relationship partner[6] here and are waiting to hear back about the best way to get a waiver and how long it will likely take. We'll let you know as soon as we have some more information and are sorry about the delay. Looking forward to getting started on this deal, and let us know if you have any questions in the meantime."*

Managing Conflicts about Conflicts and Other Difficult Client Conversations

The impact that inadequate conflicts checks have on client relationships goes beyond email messaging. Forgetting to run a conflicts check or failing to clear an identified conflict can have real implications on your and your firm's business. Sidestepping this process can prevent your project, relationships, and reputation from ever getting off the ground. Let's try to tackle another difficult situation. This one is also inspired by my own experiences.

---

[6] In a firm with multiple partners, the "relationship partner" is the partner who is responsible for managing the client relationship. This is the partner who signs off on invoices and handles any issues with conflicts, the bill, or legal services provided.

Exercise 3-1:

Cameron Counsel is in the employment litigation group at Landy Law and has been advising Fitness Feet on a separation agreement with an employee that Fitness Feet has let go. Casey asks Cameron if the Landy Law team can also help negotiate a customer agreement with another potential strategic partner, Lace Up Shoes, a national shoe retailer similar to Foot Locker. Even though commercial deals like this one are out of Cameron's bailiwick, Cameron readily agrees in the spirit of providing great client service and tells Fitness Feet that the firm is happy to help. Without warning, the following email from Cameron to Casey, with you on copy, shows up in your inbox: "Hi Casey, I've looped in my colleague here to help with the Lace Up Shoes agreement."

After reading Cameron's email, you pick up the phone to call Cameron and ask if a conflicts check has been run, putting aside your frustration that Cameron did not give you a heads-up before sending the email. Cameron says, "Oh, no, I didn't do that. We never need to in employment so I'll let you handle it, thanks!"[7] You proceed with running the conflicts check, and sure enough, Lace Up Shoes is a firm client. The firm's real estate team has been working on leases for them throughout the country. You send an email to Casey advising that you'll have to obtain a waiver from Lace Up to continue with the project.

Casey responds, "Thanks for letting us know. We're a little confused, though, since Cameron and some other lawyers at your firm have already looked at a nondisclosure agreement for us adverse to Lace Up Shoes a few weeks ago in advance of this deal, and there wasn't any conflict then. Has something changed?"

Ugh. This doesn't look good.

You do a little investigating internally and are shocked to learn that, indeed, other Landy Law attorneys were recently adverse to Lace Up Shoes and failed to run a conflicts check.

Now that you know there is a conflict, and you cannot proceed with the project without a waiver, you need to find a way to keep Fitness Feet happy, avoid throwing your colleagues "under the bus," and keep the deal moving by pursuing the waiver without delay. Spend a few minutes thinking about how you might respond to Fitness Feet and jot down some notes in the space provided. A suggested approach follows.

_____

_____

_____

_____

_____

---

[7] Cameron's (flawed) rationale was that attorneys in his practice (employment) are primarily adverse to individual employees of clients. Those individuals are unlikely to also be clients of the firm.

The first step toward resolving the issue that Cameron has created (or any other precarious client situation) is to make sure Fitness Feet's relationship partner knows that there is an issue that requires some sensitive messaging to the client. Recall that the relationship partner has the ultimate responsibility for managing issues with the client. Ask that partner if they have a preference on how to handle the communication. Should it come from you, the partner, or Cameron? At the same time, I would encourage you to reiterate that you are not comfortable moving forward until the conflict is clear. Unfortunately, lawyers may run into situations where they are pressed to move forward without clearing a conflict to keep a client happy, and it is important to be clear if that approach causes discomfort.

➔ *"Since I cannot continue with the project until this is resolved, what do you think is the best way to message the issue to the client?"*

If the relationship partner asks you to deliver the information to the client, then you have another opportunity to apply the guidelines about being transparent and managing expectations. In this case, it is also important to not undermine your own internal relationships. That means being careful about putting blame on a colleague, while at the same time acknowledging that the client is rightfully confused (and potentially irritated). This is a proxy for one of the most difficult situations you can face in practice, which is having to reconcile an issue with a colleague with an issue with a client, and come out with both relationships in good form. Remember the techniques from earlier, however, and make sure you are giving the client all the information they may reasonably want to know up front, with an extra dose of remorse.

➔ *"Hi Casey, we're so sorry about the confusion! We know the conflict did not come up previously, but unfortunately, since it has now, we can't proceed without a waiver. We'll get working on this ASAP and let you know as soon as we have an update. Since you already have a good working relationship with the other side, we're optimistic it won't be an issue, and we'll have this resolved shortly. Please let me know if you have any questions."*

Candidly, this email clearly dodges the big question (why didn't this come up before?) a bit. Sometimes being tactful and respectful of your other colleagues (even when they have erred) is the right thing to do to preserve your relationships, so long as you are not doing anything unethical, lying, or jeopardizing your own reputation or practice. If you can get your client the information they really need without having to bring your firm or other colleagues' practices into doubt, then it is often best to not go there at all. The client does not need to know that this situation may have generated some internal tension. What is important is that you apologize for the error, provide timing expectations, make clear that the rules about conflicts still apply, and do all of that with an air of optimism to maintain your client's confidence in you and the firm. Delivering unwanted news always gives rise to the prospect of creating issues in a relationship. How you deliver that news can impact the development of trust and the perception of you as an effective counselor.

Chapter 3 Wrap-Up

Strategies for Success

Writing Effective Emails

Following are some tips and tricks for writing effective emails:

1. Be clear and concise. Respect your client's time by sending an email that can be digested without much effort.
   a. Spell out any questions you have. A bullet point list can be helpful to make sure the client sees every question.
   b. Deliver any bad news succinctly. Do not bury the message in fluff.
2. Include your expected or proposed resolutions to any bad news.
3. Include any context you have around timing expectations. If you are unsure, remember the adage: underpromise and overdeliver. Overestimate how long you think it will take and then you will have a happy client if you deliver early.
4. Anticipate your client's questions; if you have the answers, give them.

Resolving Issues with Colleagues

When faced with an issue similar to the one brought about by Cameron, keep the following tips in mind to resolve tensions within your colleague and client relationships:

1. Tackle the issue directly by raising it immediately and to the right person (e.g., the internal relationship partner for the client, if there is one, and the appropriate contact at the client, such as the individual you have been working with most directly). Shying away from problem-solving does not instill confidence in one as a lawyer.
2. The relationship partner for a client should always be involved if there is a possibility of delivering unwelcome news and particularly if that news relates to how the firm has provided services (e.g., failed to get a waiver or disclose a conflict). Always discuss with the relationship partner who will convey the information to the client and how.

3. Do not be accusatory with your colleagues. Instead of saying to Cameron, "you never ran conflicts," consider merely stating the problem, taken as fact: "it looks like a conflicts check was never run, but now that it has been, let's figure out the best way to convey the results to the client."

4. Never identify the problem to the client without some indication that you are finding a solution.

Chapter 3

Sample Exercise Responses

Exercise 3-1:

A proposal to resolve the issue presented in Exercise 3-1 is set forth in the text of the Chapter, and includes the following techniques:

1. Make Fitness Feet's relationship partner aware of the issue and confirm their preference for how to manage the communication to Fitness Feet.
2. Gently reiterate to the relationship partner your discomfort at proceeding without a resolution to the conflicts issue.
3. If you are responsible for communicating with the client, then take care to manage expectations, be transparent, and avoid throwing a colleague under the bus.

Chapter 4

Efficient Preparation: Getting All the Facts and Understanding Objectives

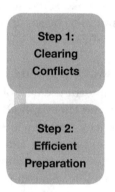

Step 1:
Clearing
Conflicts

Step 2:
Efficient
Preparation

Once you are assured that conflicts is clear, let your client know (clients love good news) and use the few details you already have about the deal to pivot to a deeper dive into the project at hand. You will need to start by going on an information-gathering mission with your client.

Even if you have lucked out with an extremely diligent client who has already sent you a comprehensive list of all of the facts *they* think you need, I still recommend a discussion with them on the phone. Even the best clients are not mind readers, nor do they know how you are approaching the project (yet), which informs the kinds of data you need to chase down. Clients who do not read contracts regularly will not be familiar with all of the details up front. You are going to have questions and follow-ups, and even one or two seemingly direct questions can result in a dozen follow-ups or a thoughtful discussion about general approach and goals.

As such, the most efficient way to get the necessary information, and to explain to a client why the various details matter, is to have a live conversation rather than trade emails over a long thread. This also gives you an opportunity to get to know your client's personality and build a rapport. Additionally, recall that your duty, as your clients' legal-educator-in-chief, is to get them familiar with the kind of information you need to cut down on future back-and-forth and to make sure they are understanding the questions you are asking and why. That can only be effectively accomplished over the phone.

Call Preparation

Once a client call is calendared, do just a little bit of prep work. First, review your firm's policy for billing to "get up to speed." Many partners do not like to bill a client hundreds of dollars of an associate's time simply reading corporate documents or running Google searches to find press about the company. I make some suggestions in this section for you to get enough information to be set up for a productive client call, but the internal policy at your firm will surely govern over the recommendations in this book.

If this is your first time working with the client, then set aside five to ten minutes to do a quick internet search of your client. A brief search enables you to understand the client's basic business, how they market their products and/or services, and how they articulate their values to their customer or user base. By way of example, for Fitness Feet, this means reviewing its website, reading any reasonably recent news articles (often found in a "press" section on a company's website), and perhaps glancing at its social media accounts (but stopping yourself before going down a never-ending Twitter rabbit hole). You may also want to take a few minutes to search the counterparty (if you already know who they are) to learn similar facts. Another five minutes should be sufficient to gain enough information that you will not have to waste time on the phone with the basics of your client's and its counterparty's business.

In my experience, the fifteen-minute (max) endeavor described earlier is generally accepted without having to seek approval. If a partner is worried about a client objecting to the bill, then a fraction of an hour is not a lot to write off, but any more than that can cause issues. The purpose of this exercise is not to uncover every dirty secret but just to orient your thinking in a mindful manner in advance of a live conversation. Clients do not want to (and will not) pay for excessive amounts of time they have not asked to be spent and will appreciate the opportunity to fill in any meaningful gaps during a thoughtful phone conversation.

In addition to your quick search, briefly pursue any relevant internal institutional knowledge within your firm. Chatting with coworkers can yield helpful data points to help you calibrate as you are going into the project. If there are other attorneys at your firm who have worked with the same client, seek them out for a quick conversation. Popping into a colleague's office can uncover valuable intel about prickly personalities as well as the client's level of fee sensitivity. It is also a great way to introduce yourself to coworkers, particularly in practice groups that you may not be familiar with. If you have this information on hand before you get on the phone with the client, then you can prepare for your conversation with the appropriate level of calibration in mind and having thought through additional efficiencies to leverage, if needed.

What You Need to Know

Having completed your preliminary fact-finding, you are ready to hop on the phone to collect all the rest of the mission-critical data needed to put together a contract (or mark up the other side's draft, as the case may be, which we cover in more depth in Chapter 7). Based on the information you uncovered, come to the call armed with a list of questions that aim to get at five key areas:

1. How the relationship is envisioned to unfold (the "who, what, when, where, and how").
2. The desired tone of the agreement and your client's relative leverage.
3. For venture-backed companies, the potential impact of terms on future financings or exits.
4. What to expect from the other side.
5. The agreement's format.

Once you are on the phone, take advantage of the opportunity to engage with your client in a dialogue about the proposed relationship that covers each of these buckets.

The Who, What, When, Where, and How

Before you can start drafting, the most crucial information to gather is some variation of "what, where, when, and how" with respect to each party's role (the "who") in the relationship that is being memorialized by contract. Who is doing what under the contract, how and where are they doing it, in exchange for what, and when does it need to be done? How exactly you get all of that information is going to vary from client to client as you learn that different personalities respond to different means of engagement and that the dynamic may change based on the nature of the deal.

Some categories of facts, however, are evergreen and will need to be uncovered for almost every contract. A sample list of questions that get at commonly needed details is at the end of this chapter in the Strategies for Success section to help guide your preparation for these conversations.

Tone and Leverage

Beyond getting information from your client about how the business relationship will be operationalized, the client will also need to provide guidance on the general tone the draft should reflect. For example, how balanced should the initial draft be? To appropriately answer that question, you also need to know how much leverage your client realistically has and whether they want to exert all of it.

Practically speaking, however, your client may not even be aware that the tone and favorability of the agreement affect the negotiation of the deal. Clients are not always going to know all of the different levers that can be pulled to advance a deal toward completion. Clients are thinking about business terms: money, performance obligations, and operational issues. You have an opportunity to add value by explaining how tone and leverage can be used to affect negotiation posture. These items are also instrumental in helping you determine how to calibrate for a project. If you do not have much leverage, focus your efforts accordingly.

To that point, these conversations allow lawyers to demonstrate that they are thinking about more than simply fighting to the death for the best deal terms possible for their clients. The "best deal" for a client may not be the deal with the most favorable terms. It might be the deal that gets done the quickest. It might be the deal that's the cheapest to finalize. It might be the deal that only has one significant term in the client's favor and leaves the rest weighted toward the other side. Illuminating these different points and understanding your client's long- and short-term business objectives are what distinguish lawyers from robots. Understanding the different options that are available to clients throughout a negotiation and articulating to your client how they can be engaged so the client can make a decision about the most effective posture to take is how you develop a relationship. Moreover, dialogues about tone and leverage also build up your understanding of how the client thinks about different kinds of deals, which *you* can then use to calibrate accordingly and make later projects more efficient.

Therefore, a thoughtful conversation about these items will show yourself to be a partner to the client. Further, if you can explain the options in a digestible, business-friendly manner, then hopefully your client will recall the conversation for the next deal.

Use this value-add moment wisely in articulating your client's options. In situations where the client has a lot of leverage, you may suggest a reasonably balanced draft in order to get across the finish line more quickly and save money on passing drafts back and forth. Do not overlook this issue or ignore your client's instructions just because it is more fun to draft super aggressively and use all of your leverage. Instead, talk with your client about how exerting leverage in an unreasonable way can occasionally backfire if the other side gets their lawyer involved. If the client asks for an even-handed approach, ask them if they want to take that position for *all* of the terms or just the risk-shifting provisions. Onerous risk-shifting terms can be the impetus for the other side engaging lawyers where they may not have if a balanced approach was taken. As a result, sometimes when clients ask for "balance," what they mean is they want balance on the "legal" provisions and prefer a more favorable (to them) tone on the business sections. In fact, if the business provisions are more one-sided in your client's favor, simply making the limitation of liability mutual can go a long way toward getting a deal across the finish line. Remember, the businesspeople on the other side are asking *their* lawyer to help them get a deal done, too. If the counterparty's business team is fine with what you have proposed on the performance obligations, then sometimes they will ask their lawyer to simply "sign off" on the rest. Make it easy for them by being fair.

If the client is not sure how much leverage they have, then chime in based on your experience and conversations with colleagues to right-size their expectations. A small start-up that is doing a deal with a giant public company and has a list of thirty changes they need made to that company's draconian form agreement may need to have its heart broken.

> → *"I know this agreement is terrible and has a lot of bad terms, but realistically, in my experience, the other side is going to reject almost everything you want to change. Let's discuss how important this deal is to you and which of the sections on your list you can live with as-is if you need to get this deal done. I don't want you to waste your time and money having me mark-up this agreement with a bunch of changes we can be pretty confident will be rejected."*

It's not fun to have those conversations. However, negotiation capital is never unlimited, and like a financial advisor, you should be advising your client on how to spend it. Most clients will value your honesty and directness. They are busy, too, and will appreciate that you are not spinning your wheels and wasting their money on a draft that will go nowhere. A short conversation that results in a marked adjustment to a client's asks will bring down their bill dramatically because it will eliminate unnecessary, time-consuming work. Also, being up front and honest about the possible reaction based on your experience is a dose of transparency that your client will appreciate, leading them to develop more trust in you.

Some clients may not believe you, unfortunately. The right answer in those cases, however, is never to simply make all the changes the client requests and send it to the other side without talking through the consequences and likely reactions. You still need to manage your client's expectations, even if they reject your advice. It shows that you are looking out for them and their best interests, not just your own.

Impact on Financings and Exits

As you are discussing the project with your client, keep in mind the potential impact on future financing rounds or exits that particular terms will have. For example, if the client agreed to a noncompete that prevents them from entering a dozen markets throughout the world because it really wants to enter into a strategic partnership with a competing company, then they need to be prepared for the impact that the noncompete could have on its future financial situation: neither investors nor potential acquirers like to see companies voluntarily restricting their ability to grow into different markets, and it puts a damper on the economic upside to an acquisition or a financing.

Similarly, if your client is willing to agree to an anti-assignment provision that requires they seek consent from the other party in the event of any sort of change of control, then be sure to advise them on how that might turn off potential acquirers. Or, your client may have tentatively agreed to a most-favored nations provision that ensures the other side will maintain the lowest price offered to any other customer. In that case, they need to be counseled on how investors may react to them minimizing the potential revenue they can obtain from that particular customer.

Last, financings and M&A agreements require clients to "disclose" contracts they have entered into with certain terms. These disclosure obligations regularly include any "business restrictions," such as most favored nations and exclusivity clauses, but can be as general as "any contract containing intellectual property infringement indemnification obligations." It is important to keep potential disclosure obligations in mind, as having to list numerous contracts can be extremely burdensome for both you and your client.

As your client's advisor, it is on you to be thinking, and get them thinking, about how each individual deal contributes to the whole of their future growth opportunities. That sort of consideration shows the investment on your end in ensuring their success.

Understanding the Other Side

Another part of the lawyer's job is to understand the other side's positions and preview any predictable reactions to contract terms. Clients are paying, in part, for the experience that attorneys have in seeing a lot of transactions and different players. Leverage that experience to advise your client on what you expect to see out of this deal.

As an initial matter, understand from the client if they have apprehensions about various aspects of the other side's business that are worth keeping in mind, if not directly addressing in the draft. These concerns may have arisen from conversations between your client and the other side or basic reconnaissance that your client did to understand its counterparty. Any live question-and-answer (Q&A) session with the client should openly address these worries. For instance, if the other side confessed to your client that it recently had a security breach and was delinquent in finding the cause, then cybersecurity measures should probably be addressed in the risk-shifting provisions and elsewhere. If the other side is cash-strapped and your client is concerned they might go out of business, then you can think about different ways to protect your client. In a software license, for example, you might require the other side put their source code in "escrow" such that your client would have access to the underlying code if the counterparty went under. Elicit these concerns from your client so you can effectively address them.

Additionally, ask the client if the other side has made any particular requests that are worth accommodating at the outset of the process as a show of good faith. By this, I mean requests that do not prejudice your client or otherwise affect its bargaining position. For instance, if Casey from Fitness Feet wrote you the following email, surely you'd accommodate: "One more thing about the draft—the other side said their standard payment terms are thirty days within receipt of an invoice, and payment must be made by wire. That's fine with us, so let's build that in." Contrast the payment timing request with the following, however: "The other side said they want us to agree to exclusivity in their industry, so we won't do a customer deal with any of their competitors. We're not sure we want to go that route." The former email sets out a non-controversial agreement on payment provisions. The latter is passing on a request about a material covenant being asked of your client that could affect its business and probably warrants more discussion with both your client and the other side and should not be built into the contract outright.

Last, consider and preview for the client any positions the other side might reasonably take, or the things they might be concerned about in doing a deal with your client. You do not need to read the other side's mind, just flag the obvious asks from the other side given the parties' relationship, the industry, the law, or external circumstances. This is part of how you use your experience to your advantage. Prepare your client for predictable asks or pushback to what you have proposed by explaining to them how you think the draft will be received. Helping your client avoid surprises by demonstrating the context that you have as a lawyer who represents multiple clients and sees issues over and over again helps build the trust you are seeking to foster. You might even caution your client that their suggestion is not "in line with the market approach" for a given circumstance. Or, you might note that more companies in the other side's position are looking for a certain indemnity or representation and warranty, which would be reasonable to give in the circumstances—so, would they like to build that in now or wait for the ask? If your client is asking for something particularly aggressive, then you will also want to gently caution them: "I understand the concern on your part, but I want to flag that the other side might find this term over the top. Is there any way we could pare it back and still get you comfortable?"

Format

Finally, the format that the agreement takes is also important for you and your client to agree upon up front. Variations in format are often ignored by lawyers and clients. Many lawyers draft agreements using the same, standard, long-form template over and over again. As such, many clients think that a standard template is the only option. But it isn't, and the format your agreement takes can have a surprisingly significant effect on how easy it is to get the deal done. A standard long-form agreement is appropriate for bespoke bilateral agreements. However, often you are asked to draft form agreements for your clients to use over and over again. Consider the following options you could choose from, depending on the circumstances of the deal:

1. Arm's-length, long-form bilateral agreement
2. Two-column bilateral agreement
3. Order form with "Standard Terms and Conditions"
4. Click-through online agreement

In my practice, we were staunch advocates of the third option: moving all of the "business" terms to an "order form" or "cover page" that served as the front page to the legal terms and conditions. This structure allowed clients (and their counterparties) to adjust economics, the agreement length, and other commercial terms without touching the main body of the contract. It also helped our clients in their business negotiations by allowing the parties to zero in on one page of terms that needed to be agreed upon. We often paired the order form with one or two pages of a two-column agreement entitled "Standard Terms and Conditions," which sends a strong message to the reader that those terms are not negotiable. Less negotiation means less legal expense for your client. A sample "order form" for a license agreement appears as Exhibit A later in this book. Items in brackets are for the client to confirm and adjust in each negotiation.

You will need to understand which bucket the instant agreement falls into. It is not always obvious. Sometimes a client wants an agreement for a particular counterparty now but wants to repurpose the agreement to be a form for similar deals down the road. Give your client a couple of reasonable options and talk over which makes the most sense.

Asking the Questions

The five topics covered[1] should help you formulate a list of questions to guide your conversation with the client. As you begin to run through each question live on the phone, do not be shy about asking follow-up questions or for clarification on a response. This is true for any conversation with clients about their transactions. You must walk away from the conversation with adequate information to draft the contract that your client envisions. It is far more efficient for both of you if you can dig deep to get the right answers and level of detail *before* you begin to draft. Even having to change something as seemingly benign as the format of the agreement (from standard long form to two column, for example) takes unnecessary time.

Some clients may express frustration with a lengthy Q&A session where they are doing most of the talking. Clients who are cognizant of their legal costs do not love to pay you to listen to them talk. For that reason, it is important to keep the conversation moving, not get diverted by unnecessary tangents, and be an active participant. Ask for more detail and, to the extent possible, explain why as often as needed for you to get the information you need.

---

[1] These are: (1) the who, what, when, where, and how, (2) tone and leverage, (3) impact on financings and exits, (4) understanding the other side, and (5) format.

→ *"I know that you weren't expecting so many questions, and I appreciate your time, but it is more efficient for us in terms of getting you a draft back on your desired timeline if we can hammer out these points now."*

As always, every time you can give context to your client as to why you are taking the approach you are, the development of your long-term relationship benefits. Having a detailed Q&A with a client about their deal shows the client that you are looking to be more than a scribe and to actually partner with them in the building of their business. These conversations allow you to ask questions about why the client is taking various positions and suggest alternatives they may not have considered, which helps them be a more sophisticated negotiator and businessperson—and therefore, a better client.

As you are finishing your conversation, it is worth noting that you will inevitably have additional questions that come up as you begin drafting. However, it will appear (and is) inefficient, bothersome, and disorganized to go back to your client *multiple* times with questions that could have been addressed at the outset. Get as much out of the initial conversation as you can, and then preview for your client that you might have a couple of follow-ups:

→ *"Thanks for all this helpful information. We definitely have enough to get started on the drafting. Inevitably, something will come up during the process that we did not cover today, but hopefully we can handle those small follow-ups with an email. I'll let you know if we think another call is necessary, but I'm optimistic it won't be."*

Exercise 4-1:

Following are the facts you were given by Ashley regarding Fitness Feet's deal with Easy Exercise:

- Fitness Feet is giving Easy Exercise gift cards for up to fifty fitness trackers. Easy Exercise is to give these gift cards away to Easy Exercise members.

- Easy Exercise will feature Fitness Feet in its email and social media marketing.

In your brief internet search prior to chatting with Casey, you learned the following information:

- Easy Exercise has not posted on its Twitter feed in at least three months, and it only has 100 Twitter followers, compared to a much more active Instagram account (7,000 followers and at least four posts a week).

- A fitness blogger recently wrote a review of Fitness Feet's trackers that was not particularly favorable and claimed the tracker inflated a user's calorie burn.

- Easy Exercise has fifteen locations in the greater New York City/tristate area.

Last, you ran into a colleague in the hallway at your firm who works on regulatory matters and had previously helped Fitness Feet with a small issue. You learned that the Federal Trade Commission has recently made some recommendations for best practices relating to the cybersecurity of fitness trackers so that consumers' personal information is not unfairly exploited.

Try to come up with five to ten more questions to ask Fitness Feet about the deal that will get you information you need to begin drafting.

Question #1:

_____

Question #2:

_____

Question #3:

_____

Question #4:

_____

Question #5:

_____

Question #6:

_____

Question #7:

_____

Question #8:

_____

Question #9:

_____

Question #10:

_____

Understanding the Law and Leveraging Expertise

It probably goes without saying, but part of being an effective business lawyer is knowing the applicable law and how it relates to your deals. Effective lawyering also requires that you inform your client if they are proposing something that may be illegal.

Lots of business contracts and relationships do not invoke any specific laws other than general contract principles, such as formation and consideration. But many other agreements, both straightforward and complex, will fall under any number of legal regimes. A common example is the applicability of state auto-renewing contract laws. New York, for example, has a statute requiring a service provider give notice of auto-renewing terms within a certain time frame.[2] As another example, pricing restrictions and overly broad restrictions on a company's business, such as noncompetition clauses or exclusivity, may be vulnerable to scrutiny under state or federal antitrust laws.[3]

All lawyers should know—and stay up to date on—the various laws that fall squarely within their practice and be able to issue-spot those that do not. As you learn more about a particular deal from your client, you may find that other areas of law are implicated that do not fall within your bailiwick—and that's fine. No lawyer knows all of the law about everything, but it is a lawyer's job to know when and how to bring in the right additional expertise.

To illustrate that point, if you are a commercial contract attorney and a client wants to grant equity out of its stock option plan, then you should loop in a general corporate attorney. If your client needs to enter into an intercompany agreement with its Irish sister company to move assets around the business units, then bringing in a tax lawyer is a good call. If your client is seeking to sell personal information about its users to third parties for those third parties to use in direct marketing campaigns, then I would hope that you find some privacy expertise you can leverage. If you are dabbling in physical or mental health information, then health law or regulatory attorneys are very useful, and so on.

Over time, you will become more adept at spotting common issues or topics that warrant flagging. At the outset, it may be hard, but trust your instincts and do not hesitate to ask a colleague. Remember that law school taught you how to think about fact patterns. If something seems

---

[2] N.Y. Gen. Bus. Law § 5-903.

[3] As an example, resale price maintenance is per se illegal under California competition laws, regardless of a company's market share.

out of whack, then it usually is, and the next step is to determine the most efficient way to resolve the unforeseen issue.

How you will bring in additional expertise will depend, in large part, on the kind of firm you work at and your client's preferences. If you are a solo practitioner, then you will have to ask your client if they have other external counsel with the appropriate background that you can touch base with, and if not, would they be interested in engaging another counsel for the issue. At larger firms, you may have internal proficiencies you can leverage from another practice group. In either case, being mindful about how you loop in other colleagues or attorneys can yield great results in terms of developing relationships with the other lawyers as well as your client.

The first objective is, as always, to avoid surprising your client with a higher-than-expected bill. As you have already learned, managing expectations about the bill throughout the project process is a key component of building trust in an attorney-client relationship. In this situation, managing expectations means sending your client a quick email to give them a heads up that you think there may be an issue and resolving it will likely involve an additional expense.

→ *No Internal Expertise to Leverage:* *"Given the tax issue associated with the proposed deal, we think it's probably best to give a heads up to your tax attorney, if you have one. If not, then we recommend considering engaging tax counsel to advise on the implications."*

→ *Internal Expertise to Leverage:* *"Given the tax issue associated with the proposed deal, we think it's probably best to run it by our internal tax specialist, [name]."*[4]

Additionally, when bringing in an internal colleague to assist, take care to avoid unwanted confusion by ensuring that no one else from the relevant practice group already works with the client or has worked with the client in the past. It is easy to immediately go to your closest friend in the tax group, for instance, but if another tax attorney already has a relationship with the client, then you have done everyone a disservice. Clients expect continuity of counsel when engaging with a firm. Using different attorneys adds expenses to the bill (because each new lawyer has to get up to speed) and eliminates the benefit of developing institutional knowledge. High billing rates can be balanced out by using lawyers who have preexisting background. Attorneys who already have

---

[4] If you are using internal expertise, then you do not want your client to be surprised at unknown and unexplained names showing up on the invoice. Get ahead of this problem by simply telling your client whom you are going to be speaking with.

experience with a client will not spend as much time on a given matter because they already understand the client's business and hopefully how to calibrate for that client.

In addition to the implication on the bill, it is awkward and uncomfortable for everyone involved if you excitedly introduce a new tax lawyer for the project, but the client already works with another one. The new lawyer will have to try to exit the situation gracefully, the firm (including you, personally) looks disorganized, and the original tax lawyer is likely to be a bit miffed that they were not initially included.

Your firm, regardless of size, should have a way for you to look up who has billed to each client in the past to avoid this sort of mix-up. Yet, in my experience, it happened all the time. One firm I worked for ultimately developed an internal "attorney lookup" tool that demonstrably reduced the number of times we ran into this issue.

When speaking with a colleague or an external specialist, take charge of the project and be direct and clear about your client's fee-sensitivity (if any) and the nature of the issue. In other words, help the other attorneys calibrate for this client so that they do not run into issues with their relationship or bill. This is easier to do with a coworker than a counsel from another firm, but you should still be diligent in sharing any client context that you have to minimize potential issues (any such issue on your deal, whether it relates to your area or not, will affect you) so that your client will view you as an effective leader. Just be sure that you have your client's permission to do so first. You cannot share any client confidential information with external co-counsel without their permission.

Playing quarterback on bill management can be understandably unnerving for some lawyers, but the alternative means risking an upset client and failing to avoid a future headache. If you are working on a small project that is only taking you three hours total to finish, then you cannot have another specialist spend ten hours on it. Unfortunately, though, this happens all the time, usually because an associate attorney has not conveyed the relevant information to other attorneys. If you are quarterbacking, even if you are bringing in a senior partner, then you have to find a way to get comfortable "managing up."

→ *"The client is not expecting to spend more than $X on this project, and we have $Y left in the budget. Can you work within those parameters? We're only looking for a high-level gut check."*

→ *"Our client wants to get this deal done and doesn't want to make a big deal out of this tax issue, but we need to counsel them on the right approach— can you spend [thirty/sixty] minutes taking a look at this? If you think*

> *it'll take longer to give the client that sort of read, please let us know, and we'll run it by them first."*

The other attorney will appreciate the heads-up about the budget and level of review desired, and it may even open a helpful dialogue about the extent of the issue. They don't want conflict either. Your co-counsel may say, "this isn't a two-hour issue, unfortunately. We need to speak to the client first, and then if they want to proceed, we might have to spend several hours formulating a plan." In that case, you probably will not be thrilled about the response, but at least you have the right information to go back to your client and get their input on how they want to spend *their* budget. The same is true if you are using a specialist from another firm. You cannot leave that conversation without knowing how long it will take for them to get you feedback (and at what cost) so you can convey that information to the client for them to decide if they want to proceed with the analysis or not.

If you are using internal expertise and your client has signed off with the additional specialist review, then discuss with your colleague about when and how to introduce that colleague to the client.[5] You want to ensure you are finding the most efficient way to get your client the information they need in the format that makes the most sense. At the same time, you want to be respectful of your colleague and mindful that you may be putting more work on an already full plate. To that end, do not loop in another attorney without giving them a heads-up that they are being brought into an email conversation with a client. Failing to do so can really stir up tension internally, as no one likes having new projects dropped on them without warning or context. Make sure you and your colleague agree on how they will be brought in to the matter.

You might find that your coworker is too busy to engage in a prolonged back-and-forth with a new client, but they can provide a summary to copy and paste into the email. Or, you might be worried that the client will have follow-up questions that you will not be equipped to answer—make sure you flag that concern to the other lawyer and discuss how best to handle so that you are not a roadblock. Alternatively, I also often found that "specialist" questions were sufficiently narrow that a quick phone call between the client and the specialist lawyer was the most efficient way to nip the issue in the bud. Let's see what happens when Fitness Feet has a potential export controls issue requiring you to loop in a colleague from another practice group.

---

[5] Other external counsel should have preexisting engagement letters and a relationship with the client, so you will not need to manage the introduction (but you may need to help manage their involvement with the project, as discussed earlier).

You and Casey are on the phone catching up about the Sporty Supply agreement. Casey says, "So it looks like Sporty Supply wants to do some of the manufacturing in China. Does that cause any issues?"

You respond "hmmm . . . it might. Doing business across borders can have some implications. Do you mind if I run it by a colleague who does export controls work?"

"No, not at all. We don't want to go in the weeds, though—we can always just switch manufacturers if it's a big problem. Can you get a high-level read from them and then report back?"

You shoot a quick email to Morgan, an associate in the export controls group. "Hey Morgan, I have a client entering into a manufacturing deal with a company that does some of its manufacturing in China. They want to know if there are any issues there but are just looking for high-level feedback at the moment. Do you have a few minutes to hop on the phone with me and let me know what you think?"

After you speak with Morgan, you report back to Casey. "Hi Casey, I chatted with our colleague, Morgan, and while it might not be a quick issue, we think it makes sense for the two of you to hop on the phone for ten to fifteen minutes to talk through some specifics. We're hoping that will resolve things. Does that work for you?" Casey responds, "Absolutely, let's set it up." Casey and Morgan schedule a call, talk through the issue, and find a mutually agreeable solution to take back to Sporty Supply.

Exercise 4-2:

You may remember that Fitness Feet asked you for a noncompetition clause in its deal with Sporty Supply. Casey followed up over email to give you more detail on what the company is looking for: "We want to prohibit Sporty Supply from working with any other wearable fitness company anywhere in the world for ten years so we can make it difficult for competitors to enter the market. Right now, there are only a couple other companies doing what we do, and we want to keep it that way so we can grow our market share. Can we do that?"

You are concerned about two things: (1) that Sporty Supply will balk at such an onerous restriction and potentially walk from the deal and (2) that this restriction may not be enforceable under competition laws. You are not an antitrust expert, and Fitness Feet has not engaged antitrust counsel at Landy Law or elsewhere. What are some steps you can take to prepare Fitness Feet for possible alternatives for both issues?

Issue #1:

_____

_____

Issue #2:

_____

_____

Chapter 4 Wrap-Up

Strategies for Success

Asking Effective Questions

Here are some common questions to use as a guideline for a conversation with a client about a new deal:

Who, What, When, Where, and How

1. What is each party promising to do?
2. How is that party going to fulfill their promise?
3. When must each party fulfill their promises by (including timelines unique to particular obligations, as well as the term of the contract)?
4. What is each party getting out of the deal (and how and when is it being exchanged)?[6]
5. Why might either party want to get out of the contract prior to its natural end date?

Tone and Leverage

6. How much relative leverage does each party have?
7. How balanced should the draft be?
   a. If you want to take a balanced approach, does "balance" apply to all provisions or just the risk-shifting provisions?

Impact on Financing

8. Discuss whether any proposed terms will have a likely impact on future financings or exit opportunities.
   a. Be on the lookout for suggestions of provisions relating to a change of control or onerous business restrictions.

---

[6] This is akin to asking what the consideration will be, but most clients will not be familiar with the term "consideration," so be wary of using it, unless you feel it is appropriate (and it might be) to explain the significance of consideration. For example, if you are worried about the lack of enforceable consideration, you might want to articulate why this question is important.

Understanding the Other Side

9. Discuss how the other side might react to your proposed terms and what they might ask for or push back on.

Format

10. What does the client want the agreement to look like?
    a. Discuss the different options:
        i. Arm's-length, long-form bilateral agreement
        ii. Two-column bilateral agreement.
        iii. Order form with Standard Terms and Conditions.
        iv. Click-through online agreement.

Chapter 4

Sample Exercise Responses

Exercise 4-1:

Here are a few questions I came up with. You may have others.

1. What is the expected term of the deal?
2. What is meant by "email and social media"? How many emails and social media posts are you expecting, and should we specify which platforms since they don't seem to use their Twitter?
3. How will Easy Exercise decide who to give the trackers to? Will it be a raffle? Are there issues with sweepstakes laws?
4. Confirm no money is changing hands.
5. Which side has more leverage (if any)?
6. How balanced do you want the draft?
7. Are there any other unique concerns that you have about Easy Exercise's business? Have you done diligence on the calorie burn issue?
8. Are there any "deal breakers" to be aware of?
9. Which locations are giving out the gift cards, or will only one location be giving them out and if so, which one? Do you want to have some control over picking the location(s)?
10. How will the gift cards be delivered and where? Will Fitness Feet have to mail sets of gift cards to multiple locations?
11. What format would you prefer for the agreement? Do you plan on doing a lot of deals like this in the coming months/years?

Exercise 4-2:

1. *Issue #1:* Talk to Fitness Feet about different ways that they could pare back the exclusivity provision to a place where it might be more palatable to Sporty Supply. Even if it does not rise to the level of illegal, you are pretty sure that any rational company will not agree to a restriction on its global business for ten years. Two alternatives you could suggest to Fitness Feet are to reduce the geographic nature (perhaps limit only to US companies?) and to reduce the timeline from ten years to the term of the contract (or both).
2. *Issue #2:* Let Fitness Feet know that you think there may be an antitrust issue, but you are not an expert in antitrust law so you would like to run this by an antitrust lawyer. If you are at a firm where there is internal expertise that you can tap, then let Fitness Feet know that you're going to have a short conversation with your colleague and will report back. If not, ask Fitness Feet what their appetite is to engage antitrust counsel. You might also let them know that if they pare back the restrictions in accordance with your advice under issue #1, then your concern goes way down.

Chapter 5

Finding and Using Precedent and Outlining Your Agreement

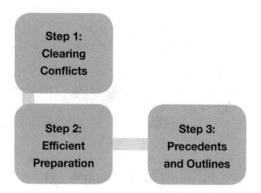

Your toolbox is filling up quickly. You are cognizant of how communication styles (particularly over email) can foster or hinder the development of a relationship. You can explain the main components of a contract to your clients. You have had a productive question-and-answer session with your client and flagged any issues of concern for other lawyers with other expertise. You are conscious of the tone you should use in your drafting language to reflect your client's leverage and negotiation preferences and have put some thought into the format the draft should take. Now, you can start building your contract.

Finding and Using Precedent

Whenever you are starting an agreement from scratch, you will want (need, even) to gather some helpful precedent agreements to draw from. Hopefully, you have begun to build up your own stockpile of documents that you like to work from. It helps to have a folder on your desktop of useful precedents you come across that you can easily access for future projects.

If the current matter is distinct from your prior ones and you do not have anything helpful or remotely on point, however, then you will need to chase down new precedent. In doing so, do not be shy in asking your colleagues or searching helpful databases (if you have access). Part of being an efficient worker is knowing how to effectively use the resources you have on hand. A short group-wide email to your practice teammates, if you work in a medium or large firm, can yield excellent results.

> → *"Hi all, a client has asked me to put together a short, plain-English consulting agreement where the consultant isn't creating any meaningful work product and, unlike our standard form, won't be assigning any rights over to us. Does anyone have a modified version of the standard consulting agreement that I could take a look at?"*

Querying colleagues for precedent is also an easy way for a junior lawyer to earn brownie points by showing a good grasp on how to utilize internal assets and be mindful of a client's budget. Sending a quick email is far more efficient than spending hours searching through imperfectly organized internal databases for the right form.

Similarly, a thoughtful search of Practical Law or a similar site can turn up really helpful precedent materials. These databases often include practice notes with each contract to help you guide your thinking. I regularly used these notes to help put together my list of initial questions for a client. They may get you thinking about different twists and turns you had not anticipated.

It is unlikely that one precedent deal will be all you need. (You are very lucky if you find that one magical, perfect agreement.) Rather, when you start drafting from precedent, it is more likely that different agreement forms will be useful for different sections, and you will need to graft your contract together from two or three prior documents.

In collecting your precedent deals, consider which forms will be useful for which sections. It can be overwhelming to look at multiple agreements and not know whether you have good precedent language for all of the sections you are looking for. If you are mindful of this when you are choosing your precedent, you can cut back on some anxiety and fill in gaps during the process. You certainly don't want to end up with three precedents that have good representations and warranties but no useful language for any other sections.

There are numerous tactics you can employ to keep track of which precedent will be helpful for different sections. One approach is to outline your contract, as described in more detail in the next section. Another tactic is to simply make edits on your precedent documents directly, flagging each section that you are going to use in your contract and noting where you will use it. You can highlight the sections (electronically or on paper), or use any other method to indicate where you are going to be grafting that language into your document and how you might need to change it. Pretend that you have found a comprehensive representation and warranty section from a precedent document that includes some bespoke representations that were unique to the precedent deal (and inapplicable to yours). Go ahead and cross those bespoke clauses out (and add a note to include anything unique to your deal). By visually marking those sections for yourself, you will lessen the chances that you overlook provisions that should be edited or removed. Remember, a good client will read the contract, and anything that looks out of place will be evident. You do not want to be in the position of explaining to Casey from Fitness Feet why an indemnification provision relating to music licenses made it in the contract with Sporty Supply. And by all means, do not forget to change the party names from your precedent document to reflect the parties of *your* transaction (yes, lawyers do forget to do this from time to time).

Outlining

Outlining, while unfortunately reminiscent of law school, is a great way to organize information for a given contract. By scribbling out an outline of an entire agreement, a lawyer can visualize the gaps in information from the client and where more details need to be thought through in advance of drafting, as well as identify where quality precedent material can be used and where you were unable to locate sample language. Any good, applicable provisions from a precedent or that have already been drafted can also be plugged into the outline directly.

Let's revisit the Fitness Feet deal with Sporty Supply. Based on what we have gathered from the client and the different exercises we have completed throughout the book so far, we can put together an outline of the contract to see where we are missing facts or input from the client, what parts we have already drafted, and where further discussion with Casey might be warranted to flesh out details:

1. **Covenants:**
   A. *General Performance Obligations:*
      i. *Trackers:* Sporty Supply will manufacture and supply wearable fitness trackers in accordance with Fitness Feet's purchase orders.
      ii. *Purchase Orders:* Fitness Feet will issue purchase orders for fitness trackers to Sporty Supply on a monthly basis.
      iii. *Shipment:* Sporty Supply will ship the fitness trackers to Fitness Feet within 30 days of receipt of Fitness Feet's purchase order.
      iv. *Exclusivity:* Sporty Supply may not work with any other wearable fitness company anywhere in the world for [10 years].
         1. FOLLOW-UPS FOR CLIENT: Discuss scope of exclusivity, including enforceability of current proposed restriction.
   B. *License:* Fitness Feet grants Sporty Supply a license to use and reproduce Fitness Feet's logo for the sole purpose of manufacturing and branding Fitness Feet's trackers with Fitness Feet's logo pursuant to the terms of this Agreement.
      i. FOLLOW-UPS FOR CLIENT: Will Fitness Feet be providing Sporty Supply with a copy of the logo that is approved for usage? Does Fitness Feet need any other restrictions or approval rights?
   C. *Fees/Payment:*
      i. *Amount:* $10 per tracker.
      ii. *Invoicing:* Sporty Supply will issue an invoice to Fitness Feet for fitness trackers that are accepted by Fitness Feet within 30 days following acceptance.
      iii. *Payment:* Fitness Feet will pay Sporty Supply within 30 days of the date of an invoice from Sporty Supply.

2. **Term and Termination:**
   A. *Term:* Three-year initial term with one-year auto-renewals.
      i. Either party may terminate the auto-renewals by sending notice at least 90 days prior to the end of the then-current initial or renewal term.

B. *Termination Rights:* Mutual termination for material breach.
  i.   FOLLOW-UPS FOR CLIENT: Any other special termination rights?

3. **Representations and Warranties:**
   A. *By Sporty Supply:*
     i.   Noninfringement of intellectual property rights;
     ii. The trackers are made in accordance with Fitness Feet's specifications;
     iii. The trackers will be delivered in accordance with Fitness Feet's purchase orders; and
     iv. The trackers are and will be free from material defects.
   B. *By Fitness Feet:*
     i.   Missing precedent material.

4. **Indemnification:**
   A. *By Sporty Supply:*
     i.   Intellectual property infringement;
     ii. Product liability claims; and
     iii. Negligence and/or willful misconduct in carrying out Sporty Supply's obligations.
   B. *By Fitness Feet:*
     i.   Missing precedent material.

5. **Limitation of Liability:** Equal to the fees Fitness Feet has paid or owes Sporty Supply for trackers provided in the 12 months prior to the date giving rise to the claim.
   A. FOLLOW-UPS FOR CLIENT: Confirm comfortable with mutual limitation.

6. **Miscellaneous:**
   A. *General:* Use standard integration, amendment, waiver, severability.
   B. *Notice (revised from precedent):* Any notice, payment, demand, or other communication required or permitted to be delivered or given by the provisions of this Agreement will be deemed to have been effectively delivered and received (i) if personally delivered, upon receipt; (ii) if sent via email, upon nonautomatic email reply confirming receipt; or (iii) if sent by registered or certified mail, five days after deposit in the US mail and, in each case, addressed to the parties at the addresses set forth in the signature block.

    C. *Assignability (revised from precedent):* Neither party may assign this Agreement without the other party's prior, written consent; provided, however, that Fitness Feet may assign this Agreement without Sporty Supply's consent in the event of a merger, acquisition, or purchase of all or substantially all of Fitness Feet's assets.

    D. *Governing Law/Venue (revised from precedent):* This Agreement is governed by California law. The parties consent to the state and federal courts located in San Francisco County as the exclusive venue for any actions, suits, or other proceedings arising out of or relating to this agreement.

You can easily see from the outline what questions you need to go back to Casey with and where you might need to hunt for additional precedent material. It is far more efficient to have all this information organized in front of you as you go to draft rather than digging through various sets of notes to figure out what is missing. A blank sample outline to use for future deals is included as Exhibit B to this book.

Now, imagine one of your helpful precedent documents, a partnership agreement from another client, B-Side Music, has indemnification language that you think is worth repurposing to use for Fitness Feet's indemnification obligations. If you are working on paper, instead of a computer (where you would simply copy and paste), then you could add the following bullet under "indemnification": "Use indemnification from B-Side license." Then, when you go to draft, you will know exactly where to look.

Based on where the gaps in your knowledge have been identified and the extent of those gaps, you might want to set up another time to chat with your client or shoot them a quick email. Fortunately, you have already previewed for them that you might have follow-ups, so the additional questions should not come as a big surprise. For the Sporty Supply agreement, you already know a conversation is warranted to discuss the exclusivity issue, so a call might be best to address all of the outstanding matters at once. If the circumstances were such that all you have to do is confirm the mutuality of the liability cap, whether Fitness Feet wants any special termination rights, and how they want to handle transferring a copy of their logo, an email might suffice. Those are more straightforward issues. Overall, the benefit of the outline is that it identifies for you all of the gaps at once, so you can knock out each of your follow-ups in one additional call or email.

Chapter 5 Wrap-Up

Strategies for Success

Finding and Using Precedent

1. Don't be shy about asking coworkers for helpful precedent.
2. Find two to three good precedent documents.
3. Use external legal resource databases if you have access.

Outlining

1. Plug in provisions from precedent materials, either verbatim or by including a reference to the section of the precedent agreement.
2. Fill in the facts that you have already and note any gaps for yourself.
   a. Emphasize items that you need to discuss with your client so you can efficiently construct a list of follow-up questions.
3. Fill in any provisions that you have already drafted.

Chapter 6

Putting Pen to Paper: User-Friendly Drafting

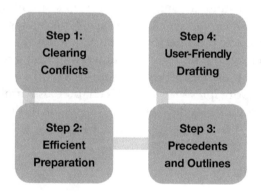

E quipped with all of the relevant deal details from your client, you are finally ready to put pen to paper. The next, and perhaps most important, task is to make sure that the work product is drafted and presented in a way that is accessible to clients and the other side without any of them having to put in much effort. In other words, your job as a lawyer is to create a final product that does not require a special "lawyer-interpreter" to understand. Exploiting your legal training to create an unnecessary dependency (i.e., to require legal training to interpret an overly legalese-y document) is not productive; creating dependency is not the same as creating trust (in fact, the two are opposites).

Moreover, remember that as external counsel (and, to a degree, as in-house counsel as well) you are a line item in a company's budget. Legal is always an expense for a company and never a revenue driver, which is an obstacle that must be overcome in building relationships. Getting over that hurdle requires that a lawyer show clients that they are looking to be a partner in the clients' long-term success. One way to show that commitment is by enabling your clients to review, reflect on, and refer to their own contractual engagements without having to call (and pay) you every time.

Therefore, the lawyer's mission is to articulate its clients' deals in a manner that can be understood by both parties, is reflective of the agreed-upon terms, and is within the bounds of the law. That is what clients are paying for—not unnecessary herebys, wherebys, and therebys, or lengthy and unnecessarily complex performance covenants. Outside lawyers have no performance obligations (and no economic liabilities) under their clients' contracts, so it really does not make sense if they are the only ones who can read their clients' contracts to understand what is required for each party's performance. While you do not need to dumb down indemnification language or draft as if a twelve-year-old is your target audience, you do need to avoid the overlawyering trap that results in complicating uncomplicated concepts or adding unnecessary words, both of which can create more problems, ambiguity, and room for disputes. Say what you need to say once, and say it clearly.

This chapter sets out drafting techniques for putting together a draft that is good and user (i.e., ordinary, professional worker) friendly. Most of the drafting principles set out in this chapter also apply to when you are marking up another side's draft; we discuss the distinctions between that situation and taking the first turn in Chapter 7.

Draft Mindfully

In beginning the initial "turn" (i.e., draft of a document), it is very tempting to get a first draft done as quickly as possible. The client (or a more senior associate/partner) might be demanding a fast turn-around.[1] You may have several other tasks to finish before an important commitment with family, friends, or a significant other. Maybe the client's relationship partner is begging you to "spend as little time as possible" (i.e., be as cheap as possible). Or, you are just eager to get it out of the way and move on to another item on your never-ending to-do list. Every one of those situations has happened to me time and time again,

---

[1] In my experience, clients (particularly younger companies) can be fearful that they will lose a deal if they do not get the contract out as soon as possible. Be gentle in pushing back as much as you need to: "I know this deal is super important so I will be as efficient as possible, but it might take a [couple of days] to sort through everything and get a good first draft together. Fortunately, if we take the time now to develop a good first turn, it'll cut down on the back-and-forth after we send it over."

and admittedly, it took me a few years to realize that rushing through that first draft did not actually pay off. The better time investment was to be thoughtful and careful about my first draft, which then reduced the time I spent editing and redrafting. In other words, to borrow my father's favorite words of wisdom: short-term pain, long-term gain.

This skill is not easy. It requires noticing and correcting nit typos as they are being made, making sure conforming changes are instituted throughout the document when sections are re-jiggered, and being thoughtful about whether the precedent being used needs more edits than originally anticipated. All of this requires working much more mindfully with a minimal amount of distractions in order to save time on the back end. But, if you can get in the habit of focusing on your drafting and letting nonurgent emails go unanswered for an hour or two, then your first stab at the meat of the agreement will be so much better.[2] Ideally, this all results in fewer proofreads (one or two, rather than three or four) after the fact. When you go back to review the document, hopefully there will be far fewer distracting, nonsubstantive errors.

A big part of drafting mindfully is thinking critically about the language you are using *while* you are drafting, as opposed to waiting until you are proofing. To be mindful while you are in the drafting process, think about the words you are using and whether they are the right ones for what you are trying to articulate as you are typing out your contract. If they are not, then make the change to more clear and concise words in the moment. This skill simply takes practice; it will not develop overnight. It requires a conscious shift in habits.

Being able to draft clearly and concisely and in a way that your clients will understand will set you apart. The following section includes several tips and tricks to be a more user-friendly drafter.

User-Friendly Drafting

Clients usually know that anytime lawyers have to get involved, some level of friction will be introduced into their business relationship with the other side. It's inevitable. To nonlawyers, attorneys are synonymous with arguments and adversity. I had many conversations with clients who wanted quick advice on how to handle negotiations but absolutely "did not want to get lawyers involved." Therefore, an outside counsel has a choice in its practice—they can either lean-in to the reputation that attorneys have for making things difficult, or they can seek to dispel that myth. This section focuses on the latter by encouraging user-friendly drafting.

---

[2] If you are finding that you are easily distracted by every incoming email, then consider turning off "desktop notifications" for emails.

"User friendly" means being clear and concise and avoiding unnecessary length or legalese. I want you to ensure your drafting is accessible to a businessperson as well as opposing counsel by writing in clear, understandable statements. Showing yourself to be able to put your legal skills to use in a way that is easily digestible by your client goes a long way toward positioning yourself as a helpful, long-term advisor. This is because how you draft an agreement impacts the pace and tone of a negotiation and the resulting postexecution business relationship, whether you want it to or not. To put a finer point on it, consider the many circumstances in which you can do your client a disservice by *not* providing them a draft that is easy to understand and interpret. I have seen each of the following situations occur, either as a result of a draft my firm provided or a draft we received:

1. The other side is budget conscious, and the value of the deal (to the other side) does not justify engaging outside legal counsel—which is very common, especially if the other side is a start-up. That company may have to walk away from the deal if they cannot understand and negotiate the agreement themselves.

2. A client—understandably—wants to be able to read and interpret the contract to provide feedback on the draft, as well as refer to it during the course of performance, but they cannot do so and have to call (and pay) their attorney every time a question arises, generating unnecessary tension in the relationship due to the size of the bill. As a lawyer, you want your clients to want to be calling you, or at least to only be calling when they need legal assistance. If they are ringing to interpret otherwise simple concepts, like the term of the agreement or payment provisions, they are not going to be thrilled with cost of the relationship relative to the nature of advice received.

3. An attorney causes a delay simply by sending an agreement that is longer than it needs to be. Length is directly related to the time required for drafting and reviewing (by each party and their lawyers). If a client wants a deal done as soon as possible (and they almost always do), but the lawyer took several weeks to draft and edit a thirty-page agreement that could have been fifteen pages, and then the other side has to spend a lot of time reviewing the draft because of the unnecessary length or complex language, that lawyer has failed to provide good client service.

4. A client is frustrated because it has a business to help run and feels like it is wasting time spending hours reading and trying to understand extraneous legal language. They begin to view their lawyer as a hindrance to their ability to build their business, not an asset.

5. A lawyer receives an unnecessarily heavy mark-up from the other side because that lawyer's prior draft was unnecessarily long and convoluted. More words and more legalese invite more redline. The lengthier the draft, the more the other side will comment on, so keeping the drafting to what is necessary, clear, and concise also cuts down on the time that lawyer spends reviewing the other side's feedback.

In each of these situations, the lawyer is the roadblock. The attorney is just "legal," a necessary but evil function that has to sign off on the deal so the company avoids unnecessary risk. They are not a partner, and they are not on the team. But, if the lawyer drafts in a user-friendly way, they avoid a lot of the headache introduced by the circumstances, and clients will come back to them more often because they trust that as a lawyer, they are not out to make things difficult for them and are seeking to help further their business.

With that context in mind, following are some guidelines for user-friendly drafting that will advance, and not hinder, getting a deal done. I have included examples for each one so you can see the difference between following the guideline and not.

Recognize When Clarity is Obfuscated by Too Many Unnecessary Words or a Run-on Sentence (But Do Not Sacrifice Clarity for Brevity)

The time-tested rule about limiting sentences to three lines on the page can come in very handy in contract drafting. If you find that your entire paragraph is one sentence, think about different ways to break it up. Dividing a run-on sentence into two or three sentences, or tabulating (i.e., dividing the sentence into numbered sections and subsections), can pay dividends in terms of clarity, even if that ultimately means adding a bit more length. Additionally, adding a defined term can also be useful to cut down sentence length and make your provisions read more clearly.

→ *Do: Notwithstanding the other terms of this Agreement, if Licensee is a party to an Event, then Licensee's obligations to Licensor will survive such Event. As an exception to the foregoing, if a bona fide and solvent acquirer of all or substantially all of the assets or securities of Licensee assumes this Agreement's obligations, then Licensee's obligations will terminate as of the date of the assumption. "Event" means a merger, sale of all or substantially all of Licensee's assets, or acquisition of Licensee.*

→ *Don't: Notwithstanding any other provision of this Agreement, in the event that Licensee merges with, sells all or substantially all of its assets to, acquires, or is acquired by (in whole or in party) any other entity, Licensee's obligations to Licensor will not be discharged or reduced (but will survive such merger or acquisition); provided, however, that if a bona fide and solvent acquirer of all or substantially all of the assets or securities of Licensee assumes the obligations of this Agreement, then Licensee's obligations will terminate as of the date of such acquirer's assumption of such obligations.*

Ditch Extraneous Legalese

Be deliberate about using a hereby, whereby, thereby, herein, wherein, or therein (or similar words). Frequently, those words have little legal import all on their own, and there are more commonly understood and used words that can be relied on to express the same sentiment without losing legal effect. There is almost always a way to express the desired concept without sounding like a seventeenth-century English orator.

A good rule of thumb to remember is that there are very few "magic legal words" that must be used for a provision to have the intended effect.[3] As such, using "thereby" is extremely unlikely to change the significance of a term or provision, or your intent. Think about non-legalese-y ways of saying whatever it is that you want to say.

→ *Do: The Initial Term and any Renewal Terms are collectively, the "Term."*
→ *Don't: The Initial Term and any Renewal Terms shall be collectively referred to herein as the "Term."*

Moreover, recall that we want our clients to be able to understand the contract they are signing. That requires us to draft in sentences of sensible length and eliminate unnecessary words. Consider these two additional examples:

→ *Do: In addition to any other remedies at law (in equity or otherwise), each Party may seek injunctive relief from a court of competent jurisdiction to stop any breach or threatened breach of this Agreement without showing actual monetary damages. Harm to a nonbreaching Party is presumed in the event of any breach of this Agreement.*
→ *Don't: The Parties therefore agree that, in addition to any other remedies at law, in equity or otherwise, each Party shall be entitled to seek temporary and permanent injunctive relief from a court of competent jurisdiction to restrain any breach or violation or threatened breach or violation of this Agreement without the necessity of showing actual monetary damages and that harm to the nonbreaching Party shall be presumed with any breach of this Agreement.*

---

[3] One example would be, as described earlier, stating clearly that limiting tort liability includes negligence if you are seeking to include negligence claims within the limitation of liability.

The two provisions say the same thing, but the first breaks up the section into two sentences and eliminates the unnecessary "the Parties agree" language. The whole contract is meant to reflect the parties' agreement—there is no need to restate their intent to agree.

As a quick caveat, on the other hand, "fixing" extraneous legalese drafted by opposing counsel can annoy the other side and be counterproductive to getting the deal done. Part of calibrating is knowing when to fix another lawyer's language (e.g., when it misrepresents the deal) and not (e.g., when it has no substantive effect). More on this is presented in Chapter 7.

If You Must Use a Term of Art or Legalese, Explain the Approach to Your Client

Remember that educating a client so they understand what they are agreeing to is fundamental to building trust and a partnership. There are going to be situations where you have to use a bit of legalese in order to be consistent with industry custom, the law, or (commonly) the preferences of a partner you are working for. I am not advocating that you subvert any of those authorities. Instead, if you do need to take an approach that is likely to be unfamiliar to a lay reader, then empower your client with an understanding of the rationale so you are both on the same page.

→ *Do: Contributor releases Company from any and all claims, demands, liabilities, or causes of action for defamation, intellectual property infringement, breach of contract, tortious interference, violation of moral rights, invasion of rights of privacy, publicity, or personality, or any similar claim based upon or relating to Company's use of the recording you submit in connection with the Contest. [**Note to Client: Even though this is a short and simple agreement for using videos submitted through social media, we have to include this "legal" language to make sure the user cannot sue you for using the videos. This is [Partner's name] preferred and time-tested construction to get that point across.**]*

→ *Don't: Assume your client understands the underlying legal landscape or industry norms by not providing any context.*

Try to Avoid Drafting in Passive Language

Passive voice (i.e., emphasizing the object or action of a sentence rather than the subject) has a number of disadvantages. First, it almost always adds unnecessary length. Compare "the payment of $5,000 will be made by Company" to "the Company will pay $5,000." Differences of three or four words per sentence can add up to quite a bit over the course of an entire agreement. Second, passive voice can create interpretation issues if the drafter does not make clear who is actually bound to perform.[4] If your contract reads "the Apartment will be cleaned before Tenant returns the keys," who is responsible for cleaning the apartment? The tenant? The landlord? A third party? By redrafting the sentence to say, "Tenant will clean the apartment before returning the keys," the ambiguity over who has the duty to perform is eliminated.

→ *Do: ABC Co will pay Consultant the fee within five days of the Effective Date.*

→ *Don't: The fee will be paid to Consultant within five days of the Effective Date.*

One efficient way to scrub your document for the passive voice is to use the "find" ("ctrl+f") feature to search for the word "by." "By," coupled with a gerund (a verb ending in "ing"), often signifies passive drafting. This trick will not capture all instances of the passive voice, but it will get you much of the way there.

Be Thoughtful about the Best Form for a Given Contract, Given the Context in Which It Will Be Used

Getting the substance right is certainly your primary duty in legal drafting, but as we have already seen, format is not unimportant. Unbeknownst to many clients, there is more than one way to present a contract, and a change in format can go a long way toward getting deals done. This is particularly true when you are asked to draft a "form" agreement for clients to use over and over again. In those cases, "user friendly" takes on a whole new meaning: can you put an agreement together that is truly easy for its users (your client) to reuse without coming back to you? The order form approach described in Chapter 4 can be very handy in that case.

Some clients may already have an idea of what they want their agreement to look like. Perhaps they want a small-print two-column short agreement that screams "don't negotiate me." Or, they do not care about columns or font size, but they just want it short and sweet. Others will need a bit more guidance on their options. Clients, and particularly

---

[4] *See, e.g.*, Brentmar v. Jackson County, 900 P. 2d 1030 (Or. 1995) (finding the use of the passive voice created ambiguity in a statute because the court could not ascertain who had permission to take certain actions); *see also* Strategic Income Fund v. Spear, Leeds & Kellogg, 305 F.3d 1293 (11th Cir. 2002) (finding the passive voice led to "unnecessary confusion and obfuscation" as to who had taken particular actions).

younger companies, will often simply ask for something as concise as possible and leave the means to their lawyer to determine, as they see length as the biggest impediment to getting the deal done. Additionally, in the Strategies for Success at the end of this chapter, there are some tactics you can employ to tighten up an agreement without losing any of the substance.

Respect Your Superiors

Last, a note on working with partners and senior associates who have their own preferences (which may contradict any or all of the above). It is not your job to change or criticize others' habits. Your ultimate goal is to manage and develop your relationship with your client. Trying to circumvent your superiors' preferences may lead to a higher bill (because the partner or senior associate requires edits you could have foreseen) and an ineffective collaborative counseling.

I worked for one partner who required that all defined terms be bolded and underlined. While my preference was simply to bold (and not underline), I knew that I needed to adjust when working for him, and that going back through a document after I had deemed it complete to underline all of the terms I only bolded in silent defiance would be a waste of my client's money. You and the other attorneys you work with (irrespective of whether they are more senior or junior) on a particular client must be on the same page and present a united front on your approach to any matter. If you are the most junior person on the client or project, then you need to acquiesce to the others' standards. If, and when, you are the more senior lawyer, then you can impose your will on others.

The Efficiencies of User-Friendly Drafting

I cannot overstate the importance of drafting a user-friendly contract. Over several years, I regularly managed my clients' frustration when provided a contract by the other side to a deal that they could not understand or that was simply too long to read and mark up expeditiously. Receiving such a draft immediately signaled two things to them: first, it would take longer to review (both for them and myself), and second, it would be more expensive as a result of the first circumstance. Neither extra time nor extra cost help move the client's business forward. While no lawyer can control how the other side will present a draft, clients greatly appreciate when your lawyering style is aligned with their business objectives.

Additionally, presenting a user-friendly agreement allows clients to spend their legal resources in a meaningful way. If clients can easily ascertain for themselves when the contract is set to expire, when they get paid (and most importantly—to them—how much), and whether they can assign the agreement in the event of a proposed acquisition, then when they do come back to their legal advisors, it will be for questions and concerns that are truly worth the billable hour rate. What is the impact of a breach of the noninfringement representation? Is there a cap to an indemnification recovery if we get fined by the Federal Trade Commission for marketing to minors without the proper protocols in place? Those (and other substantive questions) are the issues that reflect a lawyer's legal training and demonstrate their value to clients.

Moreover, if a client has a clear understanding of the draft, then they will be able to negotiate much of the business terms, such as fees and term of agreement, more effectively without having to bring in counsel. Clients can get easily overwhelmed by legalese and shut down when trying to understand complicated contract provisions. Empowering a client to advocate on behalf of itself is not a bad thing. Clients usually do not want to pay to have their lawyers sit on the phone while they discuss the economics (fundamentally a business issue) with the other side.

Exercise 6-1:

Return to the covenants you drafted in Exercise 2-3 for the Fitness Feet and Sporty Supply agreement with the discussed principles in mind. Is there any drafting that could be adjusted to be more user friendly?

Covenant 1:

_____

_____

Covenant 2:

_____

_____

Covenant 3:

_____

_____

Covenant 4:

_____

_____

Covenant 5:

_____

_____

Covenant 6:

_____

_____

For an example of how these covenants could be drafted in a user-friendly manner, please review the Sample Exercise Response for Exercise 2-3.

Chapter 6 Wrap-Up

Strategies for Success

Drafting Checklist—Tone, Form, and Language

1. Do not obfuscate clarity with too many unnecessary words or run-on sentences.
2. Ditch extraneous legalese and Old English.
3. Include notes to your client regarding any terms of art or techniques that are necessarily fraught with legalese.
4. Avoid the passive voice.
5. Consider the best format for the contract:
   a. Standard long-form bilateral agreement
   b. Two-column bilateral agreement
   c. Order form with Standard Terms and Conditions
   d. Click-through online agreement
6. Respect your superiors' preferences.

Trimming Length

If your agreement is still "too long" after you have tried every drafting tip in the book (and not just this book) to ensure the language is clear and concise, then here are a few other tips that play with form (not substance) to make a document shorter:

1. Decrease the margin size.
2. Depending on the kind of agreement, play with font size. For any standard long-form bilateral agreement, 11 is usually acceptable. If you are working on a more standardized agreement in two-column format, you can probably get away with 10, and I've seen as small as 9.5.
3. Scrub your document for the passive voice to eliminate unnecessary words.
4. If it makes sense logically, combine subsections that are separated by a line break into one section. Do not combine subsections that relate to different subject matters.

5. Eliminate unnecessary words, legalese or not. Consider the difference between "Licensor retains all rights in and to the Product" instead of "Licensor retains all right, title, and interest in and to the Product."[5]

6. Set your paragraph type to "justified."

A short example of how user-friendly drafting can dramatically improve the readability of contract provisions is included as Exhibit C. Exhibit C also includes the formatting changes suggested earlier to trim length.

---

[5] "Title" is akin to ownership, which is both a right and an interest. A "right" in something is the same as having an "interest" in something. So, pick "right" or "interest" and stick with it.

Chapter 7

Marking Up Someone Else's Draft and Reviewing Redlines

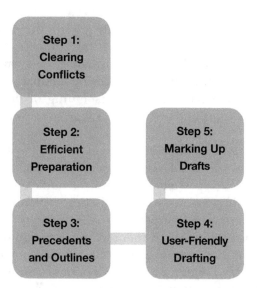

Ortunately, many of the principles discussed in Chapter 6 also apply when you are not putting together the initial draft and instead are marking up what you received from the other side—either their first draft or comments to yours. However, there are some consequential distinctions to keep in mind. Notably, if the other side prepared the initial draft, then a lawyer's ability to draft in a user-friendly way will be slightly constrained by the decisions that the other side made. We discuss in this chapter how you will need to maintain consistency with some of those choices.

Additionally, whenever a lawyer receives a draft or mark-up, they have one additional task to accomplish beyond simply marking up the agreement. Attorneys need to identify the "issues" with the draft to their client and obtain feedback. Then, they can proceed with incorporating the client's comments into the draft in a clear and concise manner.

Identifying Issues: Business Versus Legal

Lawyers regularly hear of two types of "issues" referred to in practice: business and legal. While there is significant overlap between business and legal issues, and an issue rarely wholly falls into either category, identifying an issue as primarily one or the other is key to securing the right amount of feedback. Business issues typically relate to operationalizing the agreement (e.g., performance and payment). These are the issues that usually require the client's feedback before a lawyer can proceed, such as the other side's proposal on fees, means or specifications of performance, or term and termination provisions. An attorney should provide feedback on these terms based on their experience and understanding of the industry and market, so that clients understand the range of reasonableness available to them.

Legal issues are those for which a client will look to a lawyer for recommendations and advice. These almost certainly include how the risk-shifting provisions (representations and warranties, indemnification, limitation of liability) are drafted or revised, as well as terms relating to how the contract may be interpreted or affected in the future, such as assignability or governing law. A client will need to sign off on wherever you land on all of these issues in the draft, but you should be prepared to make a recommendation or present options to your client with an explanation as to your rationale so they understand the different implications of various approaches.

Some clients may wholly defer to their lawyer's authority on changes to the legal provisions, while others may want to walk through the implications of all the options. Alternatively, the issue may be highly complex but not overly significant in the scope of the deal and unlikely to be worth the client's time to walk through. In those cases, do not simply make the change and send it to the other side. You still need to make sure your client is aware of the change and its implications, but you can do so in a way that will indicate you are using your best judgment in an effort to move things forward:

→   *"The other side has asked you to indemnify them for third-party claims that the content you are licensing to them is infringing. I think this is a reasonable ask, and the risk is low because this content has been out on your website for years and you haven't been sued yet, but let me know if you have any issues with it. I'm hoping to finish the draft by the end of the week."*

→   *"The other side's draft has them owning attorney-client privilege after the deal closes with respect to our pre-signing communications.[1] We think what they did is inconsistent with the market, so we are going to revert on the edit and chat with their counsel about it, but please let us know if you'd like to discuss. If this becomes a bigger issue than we think it is, then we can circle back and figure out how to proceed."*

Issue Spotting

Upon receipt of a draft from the other side, the lawyer's first task is to review it and then identify the issues (business and legal) to the client. Most clients who use outside counsel rely on their lawyer completely for this step. Do not assume that your clients will even open, much less read, the agreement before forwarding it to you. They are paying you to interpret the issues and present them for discussion and feedback.

Candidly, it can be frustrating when you have invested a lot of time in helping a client understand the terms of an agreement, and they still do not even open the document before forwarding to you. Clients are busy and they are relying on you to distill the issues from the deal for them. That being said, in some cases, you may find that the client is actually prejudicing itself by spending money (on you) that it does not need to be spending by failing to look at the contract first. Those cases present an additional opportunity for a lawyer to show themselves to be looking at their client's big picture by gently pointing out the cost-saving potential.

Real-World Example: I worked with one client that did hundreds of agreements based on the same form agreement. Every time they received a redline from the other side, they forwarded it to me for review and revision. There were dozens of times that I opened the

---

[1]   This is an issue that shows up primarily in the M&A context.

agreement and the *only* change was to the length of the term or the economics. To skim through the agreement and then draft an email to my client outlining the change cost the client, typically, at least a third of an hour, which was creeping into the hundreds of dollars. As those instances began to add up, I grew worried that the client's money was not being well spent and that a complaint about the bill was in my future. I wanted them to reserve their legal budget for the things that really mattered, and I was fearful that their skyrocketing legal expenses would cause them to overcompensate and stop coming to me completely.

The first several times I received redlines with such minor changes to solely business terms, I sent an email back to the client describing the change. After a while, however, I had built enough of a rapport with that client where I could suggest that they open their redlines before sending to me, because they may find that the changes are so minor, they do not need to pay me to open the draft and write a short email back to them explaining what they could easily ascertain for themselves. By presenting the issue to them in a way that demonstrated my (genuine) concern for their budget, I avoided any appearance that I was simply trying to get out of mundane work. Through this conversation, I presented some options to the client to make the process more efficient, and we settled on one that worked for all of us. I would not have had that opportunity, however, if I hadn't invested a significant amount of time in their own legal literacy and our relationship so that we could have candid conversations about how they were utilizing me as a resource.

Once you have a redline or initial draft from the other side in hand, skim through it to get a grasp of whether you are going to return a light or heavy mark-up, noting any showstopper proposals or changes. Then you can reach back out to the client to figure out what the most efficient way is to discuss the issues and get the feedback you need. Some clients may prefer a formal "issues" list, followed up with a lengthy phone call, but many will not want you to expend that much energy (or have the budget for a several-hour review project) and will be comfortable with a more casual format. Recall that you are in a constant state of calibrating your effort to be appropriate for the project at hand. That process includes figuring out what the right approach is to discuss issues. You might even give your client some options to see what will be the most efficient for them.

To illustrate the different approaches to an issues list, all described next, imagine you were not drafting the initial agreement between

Fitness Feet and Easy Exercise, but instead you received a draft from Easy Exercise. Their draft increased the gift card commitment to seventy-five and eliminated any agreement to promote on social media. Consider the three different ways to frame those issues.

Formal Issues List

A formal issues list usually looks like the following table:[2]

Section Number:	Issue:	Other Side Proposal (date):	Recommendation/ Notes:

The issues are generally organized by section, in the order in which they appear in the document. This approach is helpful when you have a lot of issues (e.g., over ten). Some clients also simply prefer a table. Any company with a limited legal budget, however, will tend to disfavor a formal issues list, given that it requires substantially more time to pull together than the other formats.

For the Fitness Feet deal, the table might look like the following:

Section Number:	Issue:	Other Side Proposal (7/1/202X):	Recommendation/ Notes:
4.1	Increase gift card commitment.	Easy Exercise has increased the amount of gift cards you have to provide from 50 to 75.	Revise to 50 unless you were expecting this change based on your conversations with Easy Exercise.
5.2	Social Media Promotions	Easy Exercise agreed to promote the trackers over email but did not include any social media commitments.	Insert social media posting commitments, per your conversations with Easy Exercise.

In-Line Comments

Making comments throughout the agreement itself can be handy if you think that the client will benefit from reading the exact contract language in order to understand the issue. Otherwise, I found that clients

---

[2] If you are reviewing a redline of a draft, rather than a first draft, from the other side, then there is usually another column that lays out what your original draft proposed.

did not love this approach, as nonlawyers tend to have a harder time discerning how the contract language translates to the issue presented, and it puts big issues on equal footing with small issues by treating every issue the same, organized in simple chronological order. This approach also typically requires that clients be at a computer to review and respond. More and more, clients are emailing lawyers (and others) from their mobile devices. Last, the feedback for each issue may come in the body of an email, which creates extra work for you, as you have to match up the comment to the issue in the contract, leaving room for error and misinterpretation.

With respect to Fitness Feet, the comments in brackets (following) would appear in the body of the agreement, either within the paragraph itself or in comments in the margins.

→ *Section 4.1: Fitness Feet will provide Easy Exercise with 75 gift cards, each for the value of one Fitness Feet fitness tracker. [**Comment: Should we revise down to 50?**]*

→ *Section 5.2: Easy Exercise will conduct an email marketing campaign to promote Fitness Feet's fitness trackers to its members. [**Comment: Should we include social media here? If so, how many posts per week and on which platforms do you want to go with?**]*

Email List (e.g., Bullet Points)

An email that lists each issue in bullet point form can be really helpful, particularly when there are not a lot of issues and each issue can be explained fairly succinctly (with one to three sentences per issue). In business contracts, this is often the case. I used this format the most often, by far, and found it to be the most widely appreciated by clients. Putting everything in an email allows clients to respond in-line within the body of the message to each comment without having to open up the agreement or be at a computer. Moreover, it lets you organize the issues so you can put the big issues up front (even if they relate to terms found at the very end of the contract) to ensure they get the attention they deserve (and so your client does not waste time reading through a list of small issues just to get to the big one that might kill the deal several minutes later). It also is typically the cheapest of these three approaches for the client.

Be careful, though, to not fall into the trap of simply writing out the entire section of the contract in the email. That is a common mistake I saw junior associates make that does not add any value for the client. They sent you the agreement because they do not want to have to read the language and interpret the changes or proposals. If they are going to have to read the contract language, they might as well just open the document themselves. A lawyer's job is to explain the issue, not just recite it. Let's take a look at what an email to Fitness Feet might look like.

> → *"Hi Casey,*
> *We received a draft of the Easy Exercise agreement. There are a couple of issues we'll need you to weigh in on. Can you please let us know your thoughts on the following?*
> ○ <u>*Gift Cards.*</u> *Easy Exercise has increased the amount of gift cards you have to provide from 50 to 75. Should we push back or were you expecting this change?*
> ○ <u>*Social Media Promotions:*</u> *Easy Exercise did not include any social media posting commitments to promote the trackers. Should we include, and if so, how many posts per week and on which platforms do you want to go with?"*

These notes clearly explain the issue to the client and do not require the client to have to discern the problem from the contract text itself.

Presenting the Issues

To emphasize these points, regardless of the format you go with, when presenting issues to your client, you want to be sure to not just list the issue, but to clearly explain why that issue is an issue (and note whether it is a big or small issue, if not obvious). Otherwise, you are unlikely to get the information you need. A less than fully informed client can only give less than fully informed feedback.

In order to explain to a client why a lawyer is flagging particular language as an issue and what the implications are in a clear and succinct matter, that lawyer must be able to summarize each change and its effect on the deal more broadly. If it is a showstopper, then say so. If it is minor and can likely be resolved without much conflict, then chime in with that feedback as well. Last, if you do not understand your client's responses to your issues list, do not hesitate to ask for clarification (you may find that you did not explain the issue in an accessible manner for them) and always offer a call to discuss.

Exercise 7-1:

Before you started working at Landy Law, Ashley had begun working on a license agreement for Fitness Feet, who is licensing some technology from a company called FitGear to develop additional features for its trackers. Following is an excerpt from the redlined draft you received from FitGear. Categorize the changes as "business" or "legal" issues and practice writing out the issue in a short and succinct way for Casey to review. Underlined words are additions. Strikethroughs indicate deletions.

Section 2.1. License Fee. In consideration of the license granted in this Agreement, Fitness Feet will pay Licensor 10~~5~~% of Fitness Feet's <u>gross</u> revenues ~~from the sale of Fitness Feet's fitness trackers that embody the Licensed Technology~~.

Issue Type:

_____

Issue Summary:

_____

_____

Section 8.3. Term. The term of this Agreement commences on the Effective Date and lasts for <u>two</u> ~~one~~ year<u>s</u>. ~~Thereafter, this Agreement will automatically renew for successive 12-month terms until either party provides notice of non-renewal to the other party at least 60 days prior to the end of the then current term or renewal term.~~

Issue Type:

_____

Issue Summary:

_____

_____

Section 11.1. Indemnification. Licensor will indemnify, defend, and hold Fitness Feet, its officers, directors, employees, ~~contractors,~~ agents, successors, and permitted assigns harmless from and against any and all claims, demands, and suits brought by a third party against Fitness Feet alleging that the Licensed Technology infringes a third party's <u>United States</u> intellectual property rights.

Issue Type:

_____

Issue Summary:

_____

_____

Providing Recommendations and Obtaining Feedback

In explaining each issue to a client, an attorney's role includes giving the client that attorney's general impression of the impact of the change and some proposed ways to handle. Clients look to lawyers for this feedback; do not miss this opportunity to educate your client and bring them into your thought process as to why each particular provision matters and how it relates to their overall exposure. Be ready to explain why the other side's aggressive indemnification asks are unreasonable or what you think makes sense in terms of compromising on a liability cap.

Moreover, teaching a client why you are making particular recommendations makes that client a better client for you. It begins to bring them up to your speed on how you are viewing changes, cutting down on the back-and-forth, as they can start to provide you helpful input immediately. That is one of the main benefits of taking a "teaching" approach to lawyering—that you enable someone else to meet you at your level. I know this is true from my own experiences.

> **Real-World Example:** I started working with one long-standing client when I was a first-year associate. After a few years, the company began doing a lot of inbound license agreements for various kinds of media content. At first, they deferred to me to negotiate and advise on every change the other side proposed to the client's form agreements other than the true "business" issues (economics, term, description of content). Early on, I took the time to explain to the client what it meant when a party asked to limit its indemnification obligations and how that would affect their exposure. By the time I left private practice several years later, the client knew enough about indemnification to tell *me* what level of risk they were willing to accept when their form contract was redlined and whether I should push back in the draft (and I could chime in if I disagreed). After I signed off on the proposed approach, they would even take the lead in negotiations and educate the other side on why the suggested risk reallocation was not acceptable, often stymieing the business folks on the other side. By adding to their knowledge base, I empowered the client to take control of their internal risk profile and have substantive negotiations over what was an appropriate level of risk for them to bear. It is because I invested in the relationship at the level I did that they stuck with me for so many years, and in the process, I made my own job easier because I had to go back to them with fewer and fewer questions when a draft came through. They already knew what information I needed to provide a good redline. When I treated them as partners in these projects and invested in their own knowledge and training, they saw me as part of their team and thus were more likely to bring me in quickly when things really mattered and trust my advice on the various legal issues they faced.

Let's look at an example of how you might tackle a conversation with your client about issues flagged in a draft on a risk-shifting provision. Fitness Feet, in advance of launching the next generation of its trackers, has been negotiating an endorsement deal for months with a high-profile singer, Whitney Beers. All of the business terms are agreed upon: Whitney will make at least three Twitter and Instagram posts in the month leading up to launch, and she will perform three songs at Fitness Feet's launch party. No money is changing hands, but Fitness Feet agreed to a sizable equity grant for Whitney. The parties have run into a roadblock, though. Whitney's lawyer is insisting that Fitness Feet indemnify Whitney for infringement claims arising out of the software and other technology in the fitness tracker. Opposing counsel insists that this is custom in the music industry. You countered, noting that this is a deal with a technology company, where intellectual property claims look different (i.e., they are often based on patent or trade secrets and not copyright, which is the dominant form of intellectual property in music). Fitness Feet's main priority is to get this deal done. They have plenty of other things to worry about in advance of their big unveiling. Yet, you, as the attorney, know that offering an indemnity in this situation may open them up to additional exposure and may cause issues in a venture financing. They have come to you to figure out a way to get the agreement over the finish line. You get on the phone with Casey.

Casey reiterates that they "really need to get this done. Is it really that big of a deal if we give them an indemnity? The risk seems pretty remote, I don't understand why we even care."

"You're right, the chance of a claim is pretty remote," you reply. "That's part of the issue. Whitney is just sending some tweets about you and showing up for a party. You're not giving her a tracker to demonstrate or even asking her to use one under this agreement. That does not seem worth our providing an insurance policy. If you got sued for patent infringement or something crazy like that, we don't understand why Whitney would even be involved in that lawsuit. She's just tweeting. So, the risk is mostly theoretical so long as we only do this for Whitney. One of my concerns, though, is that the entertainment world is super small and many artists are represented by the same lawyers. The more times you give out this indemnity, the risk actually gets bigger because if there is a claim, now the potential universe of artists that could be brought in is much larger. Additionally, if we start giving out infringement indemnity on the technology, we'll

have to disclose in our next financing,[3] so we'd just want to be prepared for that headache."

Casey murmurs, "right, right."

You go on. "At the end of the day, it's your risk at play and your call.
From my perspective, here are the options: First, we could push back
completely for the reasons I just mentioned. We don't want to set this
precedent, and the risk is not realistic on their end. Second, you could
offer an indemnity that is subject to a cap, so you know for sure how
much money you'd be out of pocket for in the extremely unlikely event
you do have to indemnify Whitney. Third, we could offer a rep and
warranty, which gets us out of the financing disclosure issue (as well as
having to provide the unknown indemnity), and hope that they don't
ask for both the rep and the indemnity."

Let's pause for a second. Why might you offer the second and third
options? Well, you are sensing your client's urgency to get a deal done,
and as part of your ongoing calibrating for the deal, you recognize that
fighting to the death on eliminating the indemnity may be a disservice
to Fitness Feet. If the client is going to cave at all on this infringement
point, capping its exposure to a known number will at least provide Fitness Feet with some certainty about their potential liability. Alternatively,
offering the representation and warranty means that you do not have
to worry about the impact on a financing process because representations and warranties of this sort rarely have to be disclosed. In this case,
where the main concern is getting a deal done without accepting unreasonable exposure and the economic concerns are mostly hypothetical,
the next best options are to either quantify the potential liability or
give the other side the comfort of knowing the technology is nonin-
fringing through a representation and warranty without any additional
headaches. Now that you have explained the alternatives to Fitness Feet,
Casey can weigh the options and decide what makes the most sense to
maintain an acceptable risk profile and move the deal to completion.

After thinking for a second, Casey makes a decision. "Let's offer the
capped indemnity approach. I think they seem caught up in the idea
that we should be insuring them against a suit, and it does not seem like
a representation and warranty will get them there. If they don't take it,
though, just give on the uncapped and, in either case, remind them of
their confidentiality obligations so this doesn't go viral throughout the

---

[3] Infringement indemnification obligations are often required to be disclosed in venture financings.

industry. And, let's both keep a note in our records of this for disclosure purposes in the next financing."

Now, compare that approach with the following alternate reality. You get on the phone with Casey, who understandably is not sure why the indemnification has become an issue. You reply, "I know, but we just can't give on this point. It'll hurt you a lot." Casey responds "Um, okay. If you say so."

Clients (and particularly nonlawyer clients) often defer to lawyers as being the "smarter" ones in the room. As a result, it's not uncommon for clients to simply acquiesce to what a lawyer suggests without asking why or what the resulting impact is. This alternative exchange between you and Casey may get the deal done, but only after you spend countless more hours on the phone with opposing counsel, eventually wearing them down to a point where they do not have the energy to fight you (if you are lucky). And, you have not empowered your client to advocate for themselves, or educated Casey on what Fitness Feet is agreeing to. You, in this situation, responding robotically without giving Casey context or showing any empathy for Fitness Feet's position, can be swapped out for any other lawyer or even sophisticated technology. You have not done anything to show yourself to be a partner to Fitness Feet's business or that you are looking out for the big picture. Calibrating for the project includes recognizing your client's need to get a deal done and how you can give them sufficient information to make the call on how they're going to get to completion.

Take the first approach with your clients. Have the conversation with them about different tactics, even ones you may not strongly recommend. Give them all of the information and context to make an informed decision, and you will get their trust and ongoing business in return. You will also set them up for success internally. In the first scenario, when Casey goes to the chief executive officer (CEO) or chief financial officer (CFO) to get a signature on the contract, it is done with sufficient background to defend the terms that have been agreed to. The same is not true in the latter scenario, where you have simply told Casey what you think is right and then gone off on your own to fight a pointless fight.

Addressing Issues in the Draft

After the client has provided feedback on all of the issues, integrate that feedback into the draft. Focus your energy on marking up the substantive changes and being careful to avoid the overlawyering trap of fixing every little mistake or drafting approach that you do not agree with but has no substantive effect. Too much red on the page, particularly for nonimpactful changes, is a hindrance to getting a deal done. Resist the urge to reorganize sections into your preferred order, or change the verbs used to signal covenants from "shall" to "will" (or vice versa). These changes have no impact on the meat of the deal and will only annoy your client and the other side and their lawyer, potentially affecting your reputation as being an easy lawyer to work with. They do nothing to show your client that you have their best interests (getting the deal done) in mind.

To illustrate this point, following are two examples of a mark-up to a standard representation and warranty from a venture financing stock purchase agreement. The substance of the changes is the same, but note the difference in approach, and think about how you would react to receiving either.

→ *Original Draft:* *To the Company's knowledge, the Company's current and contemplated operation of its business, including the design and development of the Company's products and services, has not infringed or misappropriated and does not infringe or misappropriate any third party's intellectual property or proprietary rights or constitute unfair competition or trade practices under any law anywhere in the world.*

→ *Redline #1:* *~~To the Company's knowledge, the~~ The operation of the business of the Company as it is's currently conducted and is ~~and~~ contemplated to be conducted by the Company ~~operation of its business~~, including, but not limited to, the design, ~~and~~ development, use, import, branding, advertising, promotion, marketing, distribution, manufacture and sale of any ~~the Company's~~ products, technology, or ~~and~~ services (including products, technology, or services currently under development) of the Company, has not infringed or misappropriated, ~~and~~ does not infringe or misappropriate, and will not infringe or misappropriate, any intellectual property rights of any person, violate any right of any person (including any right to privacy or publicity), ~~third party's intellectual property or proprietary rights~~ or constitute unfair competition or trade practices under the laws of any jurisdiction ~~any law anywhere in the world~~.*

→ *Redline #2:* *~~To the Company's knowledge, the~~ The Company's current and contemplated operation of its business, including the design, ~~and~~ development, use, import, branding, advertising, promotion, distribution, manufacture, and sale of the Company's products and services, has not infringed or misappropriated, ~~and~~ does not infringe or misappropriate, and will not infringe or misappropriate, any third party's intellectual property or proprietary rights (including rights to privacy and publicity) or constitute unfair competition or trade practices under any law anywhere in the world.*

Redline #1 clearly includes quite a few more changes than Redline #2, but notice that many of them do not relate at all to the substance of the draft. In fact, many of the changes made make it harder for a reader to discern what the real, impactful edits are that require substantive responses. Is there a difference between "the laws of any jurisdiction" and "any law anywhere in the world"? Perhaps there is if you find yourself litigating a case in the Southern District of Mars. Yet, because that sentence was marked up, you have to spend the unnecessary time thinking about whether the substantive difference exists and if so, if there is any impact on the deal.

Compare, also, how quickly you read through the two mark-ups. More changes take quite a bit more time to digest and understand, even when they are not particularly meaningful. The aggressive approach taken in the first redline is likely to engender some frustration, both in the receiving lawyer as well as both parties. The shared objective among all parties in any deal is to get it done, and wasting time and space on language style and preference does not achieve that goal. Imagine being on the receiving end of a phone call from a client who heard from the other side that opposing counsel is going to need more time to review the draft because of all of your unnecessary changes. Your client will be annoyed, the other side will be annoyed, and you will be viewed as an impediment to your client's business. No lawyer wants to have to defend to their client why the client's money was spent reorganizing sentence structure or adding serial commas. Those calls do happen, and they are not pleasant. Heavy, nonsubstantive redlines are counterproductive, and counter-career-building. Show value in exercising discretion, not abusing it.

When revising the other side's draft, revisit the principles and Strategies for Success outlined in Chapter 6. Each of those guidelines apply, except that, where appropriate, style should be kept consistent with the other side. If the other side underlined all defined terms, do not introduce italics. Otherwise, focus on clarity and reducing unnecessary edits. Additionally, when you are responding to a redline from the other side, it is best practice to make changes to a clean version of the document that reflects all of the other side's edits. When working in "track changes," this means accepting all of the changes prior to making your own.[4]

---

[4] Reasonable minds will disagree on this last point. Some lawyers prefer to make changes "on top of" the other side's edits, but in my experience, that approach led to more confusion about who made what change and whether it was agreed to by both parties and when. If you are working with attorneys who prefer to redline in this manner, be sure to agree up front how you will indicate agreement or disagreement to edits.

Before calling it a day with your edits, make sure you read through the entire document. These last proofreads can pick up changes to cross-references in otherwise untouched sections and implications of changes to defined terms that you may have missed. Be sure to update the header at the top with the date and your firm's name. Last, do not forget to ask your client if they want to review the agreement before you send it over. Remember, they will be bound by it and have obligations to perform, so they need to sign off on the text before signatures are exchanged. Some clients will "trust" that you got it right, and others will want to review. In the former situation, the custom is to "reserve your client's rights to review" in the message to the other side. That will preserve their ability to request changes down the line, before the agreement is executed.

Chapter 7 Wrap-Up

Strategies for Success

Getting and Incorporating Feedback

1. Characterize the issues as being either primarily "business" or "legal."
2. Determine the best approach to present the issues to your client and get feedback.
3. Educate your client on why the issues matter and what your recommendations are, flagging for them where there may be many different avenues to take to get to a resolution with the other side.
4. Incorporate the client's feedback in a clear and concise manner, reducing unnecessary edits and keeping in line with the other side's nonsubstantive stylistic choices.
5. Ask your client if they want to review the draft before it is circulated back to the other side.

Chapter 7

Sample Exercise Responses

Exercise 7-1:

License Fee: This is a business issue.

1. *Sample Issue Summary:* FitGear increased the license fee from 5% to 10% and changed the revenue base to Fitness Feet's gross revenues.

Term: This is also a business issue.
2. *Sample Issue Summary:* FitGear increased the initial term to two years and deleted the auto-renewal provision.

Indemnification: This is a legal issue.
3. *Sample Issue Summary:* FitGear deleted "contractors" from the list of indemnified parties and limited the scope of indemnifiable claims to US intellectual property rights (as opposed to global rights).

Chapter 8

Negotiating the Deal

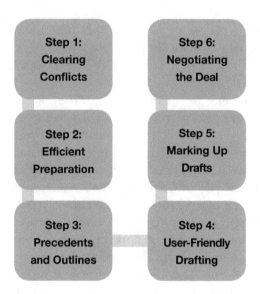

We have finally reached the last step in the drafting process before you finalize your deal—the negotiation. In terms of an opportunity to show yourself to be a partner to your client, this step is critical. You are representing your client and their interests live and in real-time to outside parties. Whether or not your client ever calls you again will depend, in large part, on your professionalism and ability to calibrate your effort on the spot for both big and small issues.

You may be tasked with leading a negotiation against the other side or just providing your client with guidelines they can use in a conversation with their counterparty. We'll review how to approach both situations.

Leading the Negotiation

If you are leading the negotiation on your client's behalf, then first, you will need to review all of the outstanding issues with your client (easily done over the phone) to understand

1. What you can give on.
2. What is a deal-breaker (i.e., what you will not give on under any circumstances).[1]
3. Where the wiggle room is for all of the other issues.

Keep at the front of your mind during the entire negotiation that you and the other side truly have the same objective. You all want to get a deal done that reflects the parties' intent and facilitates an ongoing relationship—the parties are going to have to work together after the agreement is finalized, even if their lawyers got into it during the negotiation. And yet, it is easy to torpedo those objectives with your words and/or actions. Here is how not to fall into those traps.

Be Professional

In the course of any negotiation, an attorney is representing their client, but they are also representing themselves and their own reputation as a lawyer. How you conduct yourself in negotiations will affect how you are perceived throughout the legal profession and whether your client will continue working with you (and refer to you to other companies). The legal world is much smaller than it seems. The lawyer you are negotiating against today may be close friends from law school with the lawyer you are negotiating against tomorrow. You may be on one side today, but you could be applying for a job with the other side next month. Word gets around the legal community pretty quickly.

Remember that on the phone, gestures and facial expressions are lost. Tone and choice of language are all that each participant has in order to evaluate the other participants. Even on a videoconference, nuance does not always translate well. As such, it is imperative to maintain professionalism, which I know from experience is easier said than done in many instances. But in a negotiation, much more than when you are trading drafts, your own personal character is at play. Following

---

[1] Anything that qualifies as a deal-breaker should truly be a deal-breaker. An easy way to lose credibility in a negotiation is to insist something is a deal-breaker only to later cave and compromise on it. For issues that are really important but are not true deal-breakers, you should stress the importance of the issue using phrases like "we are having a really hard time budging on this," "this is really important to us," or "we're having a difficult time moving on this without a lot of internal heartburn."

are some guidelines for how to act to demonstrate respectfulness and professionalism over the phone, even in thorny situations.

Remember Your Ethical Obligations

Your first step in beginning a project began with running a conflicts check and ensuring there were no issues, but those checks are not the last place your ethical obligations may come into play. In most jurisdictions in the United States, a lawyer cannot speak with an adverse party without their lawyer present (if they have one) unless the lawyer (not the client) consents. This includes speaking in the course of a negotiation.

It is rather common for start-up companies to not want to have their counsel on the line—as is often the case, it comes down to cost. If you hop onto a negotiation and the other side says they decided not to have their lawyer join, then the prudent response is to say that while you can listen to the conversation, you cannot be an active negotiator without the other side's attorney's consent. This will come as a surprise to many clients and be perceived as an annoyance. One easy way to get ahead of the headache of being seen as a hindrance is to have your client confirm opposing counsel will join the call before the call begins, and explain to them why.

→ *"Looking forward to the negotiation tomorrow. Just to confirm, will the other side's counsel be joining? I shouldn't be negotiating against them if their lawyer isn't present due to legal ethics rules. Let me know—thanks."*

Do Not Interrupt the Other Side

Let the other side finish talking before you jump in, even if you vehemently disagree with everything they are saying—and even if they have interrupted you (two wrongs do not make a right). This can be extremely hard. Lawyers have a natural tendency to want to break in and start arguing, and it is difficult to let someone continue saying things you know you disagree with. However, you have to let them say what they need to say to effectively advocate for their client. Treat them the way you want to be treated. It is disrespectful to cut someone off mid-sentence, signaling that you are not even going to listen to their position. Let them finish and then you can respond. If they have interrupted you, then you will look even better for turning the tables and being respectful of them. Think about making your arguments as if you were in court: each side gets an opportunity to fully present their case.

Do Not Interrupt Your Client

You may have your client join the call and weigh in on some of the more operational items, such as how their products work or whether they can accept a paper check instead of a wire transfer. I found that some clients enjoyed being brought into the negotiation, while others preferred to have me handle everything. That was usually something we sorted out before joining the call.

For those clients that do join and are willing to chime in, let them finish speaking before you comment, even though it can be risky. Clients may say something incorrect or inadvisable (such as agreeing to a particularly unfavorable term because the other side made a seemingly compelling argument). If they do, then let them finish before jumping in and saying "[Client,] before we solidify that approach, let's just quickly discuss offline after the call." That way, you have indicated to the other side that you might revert without throwing your client under the bus, and the other lawyer should appreciate the subtlety of the comment to understand they don't have a final agreement on that point.

The alternative approach—interrupting your client to try and keep them from saying something bad—runs the risk of making you look rude to everyone on the phone. You also suggest to all participants that your client was not adequately prepared for the call, which falls on you. You cannot prevent clients from speaking or saying whatever they will say, but you can make sure they are ready for the questions you anticipate coming up and advised on how to respond. Dividing up responsibility for who, as between you and the client, will be responding to each issue before the call begins is a great way to avoid having your client jump in on issues that you think are best handled by the lawyers.

Do Not Disrespect the Other Side

It is never productive to insult or belittle the other side (the attorney or the businesspeople), whether more senior or more junior to you. If you are angry and upset, keep it to yourself. Expressing negative emotion during a negotiation will hurt you and your client more than your intended target. There are many ways you can respectfully express disagreement with the other side (without resorting to name-calling):

→ *"I understand what your position is, but I respectfully think this is not as big of an issue as you do."*
→ *"I hear you, but I disagree."*
→ *"I see where you are coming from, but I don't think we can move on this because. . . ."*

The "I understand," "I hear you," and "I see where you are coming from" go miles in buying you respect in the course of a negotiation, which can translate to additional negotiation capital. In validating the other side's position, you are showing yourself to be an understanding and empathetic advisor, and that you listened and internalized what the other side said before responding. It's a great way to earn capital.

Real-World Example: I once was advocating for a client in a contentious negotiation (which had been mostly respectful up until this point) when the other side—a lawyer who had practiced for at least fifteen years more than I had—interrupted me to say that my argument was "hogwash." Everyone else on the call (both of our clients) was rendered speechless. First, by the choice of words (I had not heard the term "hogwash" in many years), and second, by the fact that another lawyer would respond to a good-faith argument with an insult instead of a rebuttal that could have attacked the substance of the argument to get to a meaningful compromise. I was dumbfounded. What would the other side think of the rest of the arguments I was asserting? Would they be making fun of me behind my back for not being up to the task? It was one of the most mortifying moments of my legal career.

Fortunately, I recovered quickly. That other attorney, however, lost all credibility with me (and my client) immediately. If your best argument against another attorney is to resort to an antiquated form of name-calling, then your argument is hogwash.

I was terribly fearful, however, that after weeks of work on this particular agreement, my client would not trust me. If the more experienced lawyer was saying my rationale was not worthy of a meaningful response, then what would my client think? This was the first deal I worked on for that client, so we did not have a long-standing relationship to fall back on. After the call, the client called me to do a debrief and mentioned that she felt the other side was unnecessarily aggressive, but I will never know if her faith in me was bruised. Both parties—my client and the other side— chose to have some business-only conversations to hammer out the remaining items without the lawyers involved. I know that was, in part, because of how the other attorney spoke to me. The other side, in disrespecting me, ended the legal negotiation for both parties.

The approach that the other side could have taken, and that you should take, to maintain the respectfulness of the exchange is to validate the other side's position before responding to the substance. What he should have said was, "I understand your point, but we are having trouble seeing why this translates to a big issue in this context." That would have been an indication to me that I needed to explain our position in more depth, or recalibrate to determine if our issue was truly an issue.

Because, Because, Because

One of the most common mistakes I saw junior attorneys make was failing to explain why they were taking the position they did. It is easy to say "we can't move on this" or "we can't accept your change," but those do not move a negotiation along. They merely state the obvious—that there is still a delta between the parties that needs to be worked out.

Explaining why you cannot move on a term or accept a change is how you move a deal forward. The other side cannot offer up a compromise if they do not fully understand your position and why a proposal is unacceptable to you (and vice versa). Have an argument prepared for every issue you are discussing that digs into why the issue is an issue, not just the fact that it is an issue.

Do Not Agree to Anything You Cannot Agree To

Just as when you are working on a draft, the client has the final say on anything agreed to in a negotiation. If a client has given its lawyer direction on where they can move on a term, that lawyer cannot agree to anything beyond those bounds without the client's approval. If the client is on the phone, then they can chime in then and there (or send you a quick email indicating their approval of where you may have landed). If they are not on the phone, however, it is not only always acceptable, but it is advisable to remind the other side that you will need to "take it back to the client" or "discuss offline first" when tentatively agreeing to anything that your client has not given you authority to accept or negotiate. The attorney on the other side will understand and likely be doing the same thing.

If your client is on the call and you have already confirmed they will be jumping in where appropriate, then encourage them to do so when discussing operational or business points. For example, if the point you are making is directly related to how your client's product works, invite them to give a plain-English explanation of the product functionality. That can be beneficial for everyone in the negotiation, and particularly opposing counsel, to understand why you are advocating for your positions. The other side should understand your client's product, but they may not have been able to articulate the details of the functionalities to their counsel. You should also be prepared to do this, but it often is more effective for the client to do so themselves.

Be Smart about Spending Capital

As discussed earlier, be sure to go into negotiations knowing which items you can give on and which you want to negotiate, and what is not worth arguing over. Many attorneys make the mistake of bringing up points that have little substantive effect (like whether "shall" or "will" is the proper construction for a covenant). Capital should be preserved for the things that matter, and then within those items, you should have an idea of how important the issues are relative to each other and how much capital you can spend on each.

In most negotiations, each party has a limited amount of negotiation capital to spend, and you often do not know how much you have until you have spent it all. This is one reason why it can be helpful to start with the bigger issues, so you have as much in the bank as possible to resolve those. If they are resolved in your favor, then you may feel as if you can give on some of the smaller ones. If you start with smaller issues, then be aware that you need to keep a lot of capital in the bank for the bigger issues. You may find yourself caving on smaller points as a result, but then you also risk losing the big issues as well.

You will find what works best for you in terms of whether to start with big or small issues. My preference was often to start with *one* small issue so I could take the temperature of the opposing counsel. If they are easygoing on the small issue, then I have a better sense of how to approach the bigger issues. If they fight to the death on the small issue, then I know that the rest of the negotiation may be difficult and I could calibrate accordingly.

Real-World Example: I once deliberately opened a negotiation with a seemingly noncontroversial issue, hoping to reset things after weeks of contentious conversations. Opposing counsel, however, was unable to shake the difficulties we had had in agreeing on other major points. He hung up on me two minutes in after dialing it up to ten for a truly tiny matter. Hanging up in the middle of a negotiation is the pinnacle of disrespect to all parties involved. It also backfired significantly on him. Although our client had all of the leverage in the deal, until then, they had been very compromising and willing to bend in places to get the deal done. Their tone changed after I reported back; they were not going to tolerate disrespect, and they wielded their leverage accordingly from that point on.

Do the Debrief

After any negotiation, whether the client joined or not, a debrief is warranted. If the negotiation was productive and both lawyers agreed to everything, subject to their respective clients' sign-off, then you might be able to handle the debrief in a quick email listing out the issues and where you landed. If you left the negotiation needing to discuss more points with your client, then you will probably want to hop on the phone to walk through the outstanding matters. Revisit how to frame issues in Chapter 7 for help in how to prepare for that discussion and describe the remaining points with your client.

Enabling Your Client to Negotiate

You may find after trading drafts back and forth that the outstanding issues are primarily business points. In that case, your client may prefer to handle the remaining points directly with their counterpart and not involve the lawyers. That does not mean that you wish your client good luck and move on to your next project. Your client may, and should, look to you to help them prepare for the negotiation and understand the different levers they can pull to get to the deal they want. Alternatively, your client may think that issues can be resolved with the other side over email and ask you to "ghostwrite" that email.

Preparing Your Client

Preparing your client to negotiate a deal themselves involves two components. First, make sure your client understands the points they are asking for and how best to position the requests. Second, coach your client on where they can expect pushback and how to handle it.

To the first task, list out your positions in a bullet point list for your client that they can refer back to. Even if you are going to have a call with your client to prepare, you should still make sure you have put something together that your client can have in front of them during the negotiation. List each issue; under the issue, provide your initial position and then, if it is not a deal-breaker, a reasonable compromise that your client can fall back to. In many cases, you can come up with these compromises with your client's input (particularly for business issues).

→ *Issue:*
  ◦ *Our Position:*
  ◦ *Compromise:*

If your client will be tackling an issue or two related to risk-shifting, then you need to ensure they understand why you are making the recommendation that you are. If you recall the negotiation scenario in Chapter 7 about Fitness Feet's endorsement deal and the argument over infringement indemnification, we were comfortable giving capped indemnification because it mitigated Fitness Feet's total exposure, and we explained to our client why that might be a reasonable route to take. Engage a similar tactic here. And, just as when you are leading the negotiation, you will want to make sure your client has prioritized the issues so they know where they should spend their negotiation capital.

Your second objective is to prepare your client for pushback on their initial positions. Clients often do not have as much negotiation experience as you do, and this is a great opportunity to draw on your prior experiences to advise your client on where they can expect to see pushback, why, and how they could address it.

Lawyers are far more comfortable in adversarial or argumentative environments than business folks. It's an inherent component of our chosen profession. Your client representative, whether in a business development, sales, or CEO role, is trying to build a relationship, and negotiations often get in the way of that. As such, if your client is going to hammer out the last few points themselves, they will value your time in preparing them for any foreseeable pushback and how they can respond. A phone call to strategize with your client about where they are willing to compromise and to what degree can ease your client's anxiety about getting into a heated exchange with their counterpart. You might even flag these items for them in your bullet point issues list.

Ghostwriting Emails

Clients often ask lawyers to "ghostwrite" emails for them to send to the other side. This may be because the clients are busy and do not have the time, or because they are worried they will not characterize the issue correctly. Regardless of the reason, the point of having a lawyers "ghostwrite" an email, versus sending one directly, is to make sure the points are conveyed correctly but in a more business-friendly tone. If the client wanted to make it obvious that a lawyer was drafting the email, they would just ask you to send it yourself. To effectively ghostwrite an email for your client, keep these principles in mind:

1. Be clear and concise.
2. Lose any legalese.
3. Write with a business voice.

Recall that Easy Exercise's draft of its agreement with Fitness Feet eliminated any obligation on Easy Exercise's part to promote Fitness Feet's trackers via social media. This is a sticking point for Fitness Feet, but Casey and the rest of the team are slammed trying to finalize a venture financing, so they ask you to draft an email they can send to their counterpart. Compare these two draft emails:

→ *Email #1: Your draft eliminated the obligation for you to promote Fitness Feet's trackers (the "**Trackers**") via social media. This was agreed upon in prior discussions between the parties and needs to be reinserted. We saw that you do not post on Twitter, so we can specify that you need only promote the Trackers on Instagram, on a to-be-determined recurring basis.*

→ *Email #2: We noticed that you removed the obligation for Easy Exercise to promote our trackers via social media. This is important to us, so we would like to find a compromise. We looked around online and noticed that you do not use Twitter much, so we were wondering if we could reinsert and just specify that you will promote on Instagram. If that works for you, then we can chat about how many posts you can make and the schedule for those posts.*

Email #1 sounds far more formal and even includes a signature lawyer give-away: a defined term. Email #2 is much more conciliatory and friendly and demonstrates a clear willingness to find a compromise that works for both parties. That's an email that a businessperson can send; the first one is not.

Final Points

After the negotiation (whether you are leading or your client is handling by themselves), it should be determined, as between the parties and their respective counsel, who is revising the draft (if need be). Regardless of who "has the pen" in making the initial revisions, you will need to ensure that the updated draft matches the resolutions agreed upon in the negotiation, that you have fleshed out any questions with your client, and that there are no outstanding issues, just as we went over in Chapters 4 and 7.

Chapter 8 Wrap-Up

Strategies for Success

Leading the Negotiation

1. Work with your client to determine:
   a. What you can give on.
   b. What is a deal-breaker.
   c. Where the wiggle room is for all of the other issues.
2. Be professional: avoid interruptions and insults.
3. Spend your negotiation capital wisely, and don't sweat the small stuff too much.
4. Debrief with your client.

Enabling Your Client to Negotiate

1. List out issues with your position and potential compromises for your client.
2. Prioritize the issues.
3. Flag any positions that are likely to get pushback from the other side.
4. Use a business voice to ghostwrite any emails.

Chapter 9

Final Tips and Tricks for Success

C ongratulations! You've worked your way through a drafting project and in the process laid the foundation for a long-lasting relationship with your client. While you will make some tweaks along the way depending on what works best for you and your different clients as you incorporate these skills into your practice, you will also find that developing institutional knowledge will help your client see you as part of their team, not just a line item on the budget.

We are finishing here with a hodgepodge of some final tips and tricks for success to use as you build your career. Some will be variations on themes already presented throughout the book, and others are more discrete skills to have on hand. Enjoy!

Tips and Tricks

Be Mindful of the Language You Use

You are going to have conversations with clients where they propose wacky and off-market (and sometimes illegal, unbeknownst to them) ideas. You will have junior associates working for you who take approaches you disagree with. You will negotiate with opposing counsel who is making nonsensical arguments. In each of these situations, you have a choice about how you indicate your disagreement or alternate views. You can be a jerk, or not. I recommend the latter.

Over the years, I have leaned on tips about having difficult conversations or communicating disagreement from the cognitive behavioral therapy field, which suggests being gentle and validating in your language, and showing interest in what the other side is saying by actively listening. I was also blessed with mentors who knew how to deliver effective feedback and have tried to mirror their techniques:

→ *"I see why you might take that approach [shows interest and validates other side]. Here is an alternate method we also see in the market [gentle manner of demonstrating other options]."*

→ *"I noticed that you used precedent A to put this agreement together. I think there might be more on-point precedent agreements in our files, so can we talk through your thought process?"*

→ *"I saw that you reverted to your prior position in the redline. Can you help me understand why this is a sticking point for you, and then we'll explain why we are having trouble agreeing with it?"*

Using lead-ins like "I saw" or "I noticed" soften the blow of an otherwise direct question or criticism without resorting to passive language or shying away from the issue. When you are more gentle with your language, you are more likely to get a productive response from the other side.

In contrast, in both the second and third examples, you could eliminate the question and make blunt statements, but notice how the tone changes:

→ *"I noticed that you used precedent A to put this agreement together. I think there might be more on-point precedent agreements in our files. Let's talk through this."*

→ *"I saw that you reverted to your prior position in the latest redline. We need to understand why this is a sticking point for you, because we are having trouble agreeing with it."*

When you make the effort to ask a question, you are signaling that the other party to the conversation is still a meaningful contributor, and that you want to learn what their thinking process is or how they came to the conclusion they did. With that information, you can learn in order to be a better mentor, advocate, and counselor.

Manage Your Client's Timing Expectations

Managing your clients' expectations of you is critical to staying sane while practicing law. A high billing rate comes with high expectations. Clients are paying hundreds of dollars an hour; they expect services commensurate with your rate. Issues arise, however, in a few different ways:

1. You can't meet your client's expectations because they are objectively unreasonable.
   a. "We need this seventy-page agreement drafted in an hour!"

2. You can't meet your client's expectations, which are objectively reasonable, due to other things on your plate.
   a. "We need a form license agreement drafted in the next two days." You have been billing eighteen hours a day on a fast-paced, high-profile $3 billion M&A transaction and there are no signs of it letting up.
3. You can't meet your client's expectations because you have an outright scheduling conflict.
   a. "We need you to get on a call tomorrow at 3 p.m. with the other side to negotiate." You already have another client call scheduled at that time.
4. You can't meet your client's expectations because you need to run your response by a partner who is out of the office and you do not know how often they are checking their email.

And so on. You are never going to be able to meet every client demand on their schedule, but you are always going to be able to reset their expectations. Recall what we went over in Chapter 3 about framing your communications with your client. Acknowledge the request, and then level set with them on realistic timing. Your credibility, in large part, is a product of how well you manage others' expectations of you.

→ *"Thanks for the note and glad to hear things with the other side are progressing. Unfortunately, I have a conflict at that time, but am free at the following times: [List]."*

→ *"Thanks for the note and glad to hear you are moving forward with this project. Unfortunately, I think I'll need a bit more time to think through and effectively paper the deal. I'll aim to have a draft to you by [date]. Let me know if that causes any issues."*

Each of these examples shows situations where you simply cannot accommodate the client's request on their desired timeline. It is totally fair in each of those circumstances to push back with a time frame that works more reasonably for you. Just do not abuse the practice of pushing back so much that your client does not see you as a partner. If you can accommodate without much heartburn, then try your best to do so. It is the times that you do that allow you more leeway when you can't.

And moreover, these exchanges will build trust, even when you are pushing back, if you then meet the deadline that you proposed. If you have the opportunity to set your own deadline, then you need to meet it (and ideally be early). Underpromising and overdelivering can be extremely effective in helping you manage your client's expectations while also enhancing your relationship.

Manage Your Client's Billing Expectations

Many times, the person whom you are corresponding with at the client is not the same person who is reviewing the bill. Or, for younger companies, the client has never worked with outside counsel before and does not fully appreciate that every time they call you, even if the call is just five minutes, they are going to be billed.

You, however, know all of this information and can help them calibrate to understand when a call is truly warranted. And, while you do not need to remind your client that you are billing them every time you talk, you can help manage their expenses using the following tricks:

1. If a client emails you asking for a phone call, make sure you know what the subject matter will be before you hop on the phone. If it is just a quick question, then you can solve it with an email.
   → *"Thanks for the email. This seems like a small question, so it is probably more efficient to handle over email. [INSERT RESPONSE]. If you have any questions, let me know and then we can find some time to talk."*
2. If a client seems to be overly worried about something you do not find all that problematic (and as a result, is causing a conversation or email exchange to go on longer than needed), gently reset their level of concern.
   → *"I understand you are concerned, but I don't think this is a huge issue and the risk is pretty low if things go haywire. Why don't we do X, Y, and Z and see if that solves it?"*
3. If the client is asking for work product that will take a lot of time, and you could convey the same information in a more efficient manner, then just tell them.
   → *"We could definitely put together a full memo for you discussing this contract provision and researching relevant authority, but we want to caution that it will take quite a bit of time, and as a result, could get pricey (we estimate around [$XX,XXX]). It is probably more efficient for us to send you a short analysis over email and then we can schedule a call to chat through some of the details. What do you prefer?*

Calibrate, Calibrate, Calibrate

Delivering the perfect work product is not the same as delivering perfect client service. Perfect client service means delivering a solid work product on a time frame that is appropriate to spend on the given project without overwhelming the client's budget and/or taking too long to complete. Take a minute or two before diving in to think about how long makes sense to spend on the project. If you are not sure and have a trusted, more senior colleague you can ask, then do so.

Be Mindful of When You Send Emails

A nonurgent email on the weekend is an interruption—whether it is to your client, your colleague, your supervisor, or the other side.

> **Real-World Example:** A colleague once told me that the general counsel of a popular "unicorn" start-up responded to a nonurgent Saturday email with "Thanks for the heads up. In the future, please don't email me on the weekend if it's not an emergency."

Weekends are time for people to see family and friends, recharge from the days behind them, and prepare for the week ahead. While many professionals work on weekends—whether in law, finance, or at a start-up—the urge to embrace weekend work seems to plague lawyers more than most.

If you are tempted to get an email out, just to tick an item off your to-do list, then consider using the "delay delivery" (on Outlook) or "schedule send" (on Gmail) functionalities so the email is not received until Monday morning. That will let you cross the task off your list without interrupting someone else's personal time.

Be Responsive

So much of building a practice and relationship with clients is simply being responsive. This does not mean saying yes to every client request and then staying up all night, every night, to accommodate. It does not mean dropping everything to chase down answers to your client's questions immediately upon receipt of an email. Being responsive means acknowledging the request and letting the client know how best you can accommodate. This latter skill is part of calibration. Some requests, given their nature, will require immediate attention. Many others will not require it, but your client will ask for it. In those cases, do not simply ignore the email or voicemail. Respond to the client and let them know that you received the message, you are taking a look, and you will get back to them within a particular time frame.

Proofread Your Work . . .

You will not always have all the answers or feedback from your client, and blanks may need to be filled in, but a polished draft free of typos and formatted logically can build credibility and inspire confidence in you (from both the other side and your client's standpoint), even if the substance is not yet fully baked.

. . . And Trust Your Proofreading Skills

It is easy to get in the habit of reviewing your work multiple times in an effort to produce what is ultimately the most perfect work product. As lawyers, we are easily scared that we have missed *something*. Unfortunately, though, there comes a point when the cost to your client of each extra review, however, outweighs the benefit. For clients with limited legal budgets, perfect can certainly be the enemy of done and good enough. If you did your prep work competently to nail the legal issues and put together a good first draft (self-critiquing and editing as you write), then aim to review two times: one for typos and grammatical errors and one for substance.[1] If you do these two proofreads well, really thinking through the draft as you read, then trust that you have done a good job and can ship the document out the door.

Don't Second-Guess Senior Attorneys

As discussed in Chapter 6, you are not always going to agree with the attorneys you are working for. You may not think the precedent they recommended is effective, or you believe that they are taking an inefficient path to getting a client an answer. It is perfectly acceptable to ask your superior why they are recommending the precedent or taking that particular path, and it may help you even come around to agreeing with them. It is not okay to simply ignore their will. If you still disagree after chatting, then instead of simply subverting their directions, you should present your alternative—your *better* precedent material or *more* efficient path—for discussion. You may find that the other attorney agrees with you, or that they don't and explain to you why. Use the disagreement as a learning opportunity.

Don't Let Email Threads Get Out of Control

As we saw when we reviewed conflicts checks, long and drawn-out email threads can be inefficient and counterproductive. Do your part to put all of the information you have in one email, and then if the thread continues for more than four or five emails on the same issue, consider suggesting a call. At that point, it is more productive to have a live conversation.

At the same time, be careful about sending too many emails that have no real content. If a client replies to your email with "sounds good" or

---

[1] This is a guideline, not a hard rule. Some long and complex agreements may require more than two reads—and due to the nature of the agreement, the extra proofread is justified. Some short and simple agreements may be able to be completed in one review.

"go ahead with that approach," then you do not need to continue the conversation unless you have something substantive to add. Responding with "great" or "thanks" to those emails just clutters inboxes.

Be Mindful of the CC Line

In an increasingly email-dependent world, people have a tendency to overuse the CC line, copying in anyone who might remotely be interested in the topic at hand. However, as a lawyer, you have ethical duties to not disclose client confidential information to nonclients, so be sure to double-check the CC line every time to make sure only internal folks are listed. If there are external folks, then email your client asking why they were copied and what their roles are. Do not just blindly hit "reply all."

Additionally, be cognizant of who is copied from within the client and the sensitivity of the information you are working with. A lower-level employee may have been copied into an email chain with the executive team early on to chime in on some operational items, but if the conversation gets more strategic and high level, it may no longer be appropriate for that individual to be privy to the exchange you are having with the executives.

Do Not Shift Blame or Hide Mistakes

This one is pretty simple. You are going to leave a typo in an agreement at some point in your life. It happens to everyone from the most junior associate to the most senior partner. If a client or the other side spots the typo, just own it, fix it, and move on. No need to dwell.

Avoid Future Headaches

As we set out in the beginning of this book, there will be many times you can foresee an issue down the road and have the capacity to stop it from occurring. Taking the extra time to avoid the future headache will pay dividends—it saves you from having to deal with the actual headache as well as demonstrates to your clients and colleagues that you are thinking about long-term consequences and potential reactions.

Exhibit A: Sample Order Form

License Agreement

Order Form

This License Agreement (the "**Agreement**") is between Company A and Company B and dated as of the Effective Date below. The Agreement consists of this Order Form and the Standard Terms and Conditions attached as Exhibit A. In the event of a conflict between the Standard Terms and Conditions and this Order Form, this Order Form will govern to the extent of the conflict.

Effective Date:	_____, 202X ("**Effective Date**").
Term:	[12] months (the "**Initial Term**"). After the Initial Term, this Agreement will renew automatically for successive [12]-month terms (each, a "**Renewal Term**") until either party provides notice of nonrenewal to the other party at least [60] days prior to the end of the Initial Term or then-current Renewal Term. The Initial Term and all Renewal Terms are the "**Term**."
Territory:	Worldwide (the "**Territory**").
Licensed Content:	[Describe] (the "**Licensed Content**").
Fee:	[$] (the "**Fee**").
Exclusivity:	[Describe, if any]
Other Terms:	[Include any other terms that vary from the Standard Terms].

Company A: Company B:

By: _____   By: _____

Name: _____   Name: _____

Title: _____   Title: _____

Exhibit B: Sample Outline

1. **Covenants:**
   a. *General Performance Obligations:*
   b. *Any Licenses:*
   c. *Fees/Payment or Other Consideration:*
      i. *Amount:*
      ii. *Invoicing:*
      iii. *Payment:*
   d. *FOLLOW-UPS FOR CLIENT:*
2. **Term and Termination:**
   a. *Term:*
   b. *Termination Rights:*
   c. *FOLLOW-UPS FOR CLIENT:*
3. **Representations and Warranties:**
   a. *By Party A:*
   b. *By Party B:*
   c. *FOLLOW-UPS FOR CLIENT:*
4. **Indemnification:**
   a. *By Party A:*
   b. *By Party B:*
   c. *FOLLOW-UPS FOR CLIENT:*
5. **Limitation of Liability:**
   a. *Cap:*
   b. *Exclusions:*
   c. *FOLLOW-UPS FOR CLIENT:*

6. Miscellaneous:
  a. *General (integration, amendment, waiver, severability, etc.):*
  b. *Notice:*
  c. *Assignability:*
  d. *Governing Law/Venue:*
  e. *FOLLOW-UPS FOR CLIENT:*

Exhibit C: User-Friendly Drafting—Excerpt from a Nondisclosure Agreement
Original

A. *Definition.* "**Confidential Information**" means:

    i. any information disclosed (directly or indirectly) by Discloser to Recipient pursuant to this Agreement that is in written, graphic, machine-readable, or other tangible form (including, without limitation, research, product plans, products, services, equipment, customers, markets, software, inventions, discoveries, ideas, processes, designs, drawings, formulations, specifications, product configuration information, marketing and finance documents, prototypes, samples, and data sets) and is marked "Confidential," "Proprietary" or in some other manner to indicate its confidential nature; and

    ii. oral information disclosed (directly or indirectly) by Discloser to Recipient pursuant to this Agreement; provided that such information is designated as confidential at the time of its initial disclosure and reduced to a written summary by Discloser that is marked in a manner to indicate its confidential nature and delivered to Recipient within thirty (30) days after its initial disclosure.

B. *Exceptions.* Confidential Information shall not, however, include any information that:

    i. was publicly known or made generally available without a duty of confidentiality prior to the time of disclosure by Discloser to Recipient;

    ii. becomes publicly known or made generally available without a duty of confidentiality after disclosure by Discloser to Recipient through no wrongful action or inaction of Recipient;

    iii. is in the rightful possession of Recipient without confidentiality obligations at the time of disclosure by Discloser to Recipient as shown by Recipient's then-contemporaneous written files and records kept in the ordinary course of business;

    iv. is obtained by Recipient from a third party without an accompanying duty of confidentiality and without a breach of such third party's obligations of confidentiality; or

    v. is independently developed by Recipient without use of or reference to Discloser's Confidential Information, as shown by written records and other competent evidence prepared contemporaneously with such independent development.

User-Friendly Drafting

A. *Definition.* "**Confidential Information**" means any:

    i. visual, machine-readable, or other tangible information that Discloser discloses (directly or indirectly) to Recipient under this Agreement that is marked as "Confidential" or "Proprietary" (or with a similar indication of its confidential nature), including[1] research, product and product plans, equipment, software, inventions, ideas, designs, drawings, formulations, specifications, marketing and finance documents, prototypes, samples, and data sets;[2] and

    ii. oral information that Discloser discloses (directly or indirectly) to Recipient under this Agreement that Discloser (1) designates as "confidential" at the time of the initial disclosure and (2) reduces to a written summary that is marked as described in subsection (i) and delivered to Recipient within 30 days after its initial disclosure.

---

[1] To ensure that "including" is interpreted as meaning "including, without limitation," the drafter can include an interpretive provision in the "boilerplate" that states as much.

[2] I eliminated a number of things from the list that were captured by other terms: services, discoveries, product configuration information, processes, customers, and markets.

B. *Exceptions.* However, Confidential Information does not include any information that:

    i. is publicly known or made generally available without confidentiality obligations prior to Discloser's disclosure to Recipient;

    ii. becomes publicly known or made generally available without confidentiality obligations after Discloser's disclosure to Recipient without Recipient's wrongful action or inaction;

    iii. is in Recipient's rightful possession without confidentiality obligations at the time of Discloser's disclosure to Recipient as shown by Recipient's then-contemporaneous written, ordinary-course records;

    iv. Recipient obtains from a third party without accompanying confidentiality obligations and without a breach of that third party's confidentiality obligations; or

    v. Recipient independently develops without using Discloser's Confidential Information, as shown by Recipient's written records and other then-contemporaneous evidence.

Thank You

I began this book by stating that it is about relationships. I was drawn to writing about the "human" aspect of the lawyer/client dynamic because my relationships are what motivated me to continue building my skills and putting in the hours, even on the days when it was very hard to find joy in the job. My bonds with my colleagues and clients made those difficult days manageable. I am eternally grateful for the friendships I developed during my time at Wilson Sonsini and Cooley, which are (fortunately) too numerous to list.

I thank each and every attorney, administrative staff member, and paralegal that I have worked with and learned from, but especially those who taught me to "calibrate" and encouraged me to find fun and humor in the day-to-day—Barath Chari, Jamie Clessuras, Gary Greenstein, TJ Graham, Rachel Mollon, and Sriram Krishnamurthy. I also owe a massive thanks to those who lent their (nonbillable) time and effort to provide feedback on this book: Barath Chari, Christina Oshan, Mark Holloway, Allegra Sachs, Scott McKinney, TJ Graham, Misasha Graham, and Jeff Ung. I am forever in debt.

Index

Note: Page numbers with n indicate footnotes.